Free Rein Series

Free Reign

Christine Meunier

Free Rein Series
Free Reign

by Christine Meunier

National Library of Australia Cataloguing-in-Publication Data

Meunier, Christine

Free Reign

1st ed. 2014

ISBN – 978-0-9875332-7-2 (pbk.)

Cover design by Metuschaël and Christine Meunier
Cover photo by Cait O'Pray with thanks to Blinkbonnie Equestrian Centre

Foreword

I am excited to be able to offer the third book in the *Free Rein* series for reading!

As with the first two books in the series, I pray that *Free Reign* will be a source of entertainment, encouragement and enlightenment for many readers in the years to come. I hope that you will enjoy reading it and learn from it, as much as *New Beginnings* and *In Pursuit of a Horse*.

Christine

Free Rein Series

1. New Beginnings
2. In Pursuit of a Horse
3. Free Reign
4. Learning to Fall
5. A Dollar Goes a Long Way
6. Contagious
7. Broken

Also by Christine Meunier

Horse Country – A World of Horses

B and B

The Thoroughbred Breeders Series

1. New Blood
2. No Hoof, No Horse
3. Recessive
4. Breakover
5. Focus
6. Yearling Sales
7. Grace

Free Rein: Free Reign

One

"Last one to the end of the paddock has to untack for all of us!" Geordie Smith called out suddenly, pushing her chestnut mare Rose into a gallop.

Caught unawares, Hannah Johnston and Jacqui King quickly raced after their close friend. Although Geordie had a head start, Hannah's taller gelding Jasper took longer strides and managed to just overtake the mare by the end of the paddock. Jacqui's smaller bay pony put in a gallant effort but wasn't able to catch up to the two in front of him.

The three girls laughed as they reached the end, a little breathless.

"That was great!" Geordie gushed out.

Jacqui nodded.

"You totally cheated though," Hannah informed her red headed friend.

Geordie looked at her in surprise.

"How?"

"By not giving us any warning!"

"Of course I did. I told you the last one would have to untack all of our horses, how is that not warning you?"

Hannah frowned whilst Jacqui laughed.

"I guess we did follow after she said that... so maybe we can't say that Geordie cheated, Hannah."

Geordie grinned in triumph.

"There! If Jacqui says I didn't cheat then I didn't."

"It's a matter of opinion," Hannah huffed, nudging Jasper into a walk back towards the tie up area on the property.

"Well in my *opinion*," Geordie quoted her friend with a fiery attitude, "your attitude stinks! You won, isn't that a good thing?"

Hannah nodded her head with a smile.

"That's true," she stated, a little smugly.

Jacqui shook her head and smiled. Her two closest friends were so competitive at times! She patted Matty's neck, thankful that the little pony hadn't resisted a gallop across the freeway paddock.

It was April school holidays and the three girls had been riding nearly every day of the week. Jacqui's mother Kate – who ran the agistment property – had insisted that the girls give their ponies a day off once or twice a week. They had reluctantly agreed to this, perhaps only because they were suitably distracted on Sundays with Geordie and Jacqui being at Church and on Wednesdays because it was a designated study day.

All three girls were in their final year of primary school and found they had been given a lot of homework to do over the first term holidays. The year prior they had set aside an afternoon a week for Jacqui to help Geordie keep on top of her schoolwork. It had been the only way for Geordie to secure a pony of her own.

Since then the girls had decided it was better to keep this tradition going, just in case Geordie's grades slipped and her parents took Rose away from her. Geordie hadn't seen the need to continue to put in so much time with her schoolwork after her parents had agreed to get her a pony, but Jacqui's suggestion that a drop in school work may mean her pony got taken away had been incentive enough to continue the tradition of getting her school work done halfway through the week.

Geordie and Hannah had been bought their ponies at the start of the year. When Jacqui had travelled with them to Hannah's Aunt Jan who bred and trained ponies, she'd fallen in love with a little bay gelding called Matty. As soon as Jacqui had a growth spurt, she would be too tall to ride Matty, so her parents had organised to lease him, knowing they could return him to Jan once Jacqui grew taller.

For now the young blonde was so excited at the idea of having a pony of her own to love. What made it even better was that her two best friends were able to keep their ponies at her parent's place.

Kate King had offered the girls a chance to keep their horses at the property Genesis for free, as long as they helped out around the property for a number of hours each week. It meant that all three took great pride in their horses and where they kept them – it had worked out well.

That night Jacqui took great delight in telling her father about the race the three had taken across the paddock. Tony listened half heartedly, responding with as much enthusiasm as he could muster. Jacqui didn't seem to notice. Kate was glad for a chance to address her husband once their two children had gone to bed for the evening.

"Bad day at work?" she asked knowingly.

Tony nodded and sighed, stretching out on the couch in the lounge room.

"I'm trying to give this new manager the respect she deserves but I'm not sure about how she approaches people or situations. We had a one-on-one meeting today to discuss my role and her perception on things. This went ok I thought. But then she followed it up with an email indicating what we'd discussed and agreed upon in her view. She had the audacity to state in the email that I'd agreed to a few actions that she was planning to take for our team when in fact I hadn't.

"I emailed her back to indicate that I did not agree to a couple of the statements at all. Her responding email wasn't a happy one. I'm not sure if we've misunderstood each other and she genuinely felt we were on the same page, or if she's trying to manipulate me into her way of thinking."

"Did she say something similar in the email?"

"Not really. She just indicated that she was disappointed that I hadn't voiced my concerns in person. Is it cynical to think she doesn't want a paper trail of people disagreeing with her decisions?"

Kate sat quietly for a moment, sensing her husband's authentic discomfort.

"I think God prompts us at times about people's characters. Perhaps we should pray tonight that you will be respectful to your new boss, but that your mind would be clear when it comes to dealing with her. It's not fair to have a prejudiced view, but if it is in her character to manipulate people, it'd be good to know that your eyes are open."

Tony nodded and kissed his wife on the forehead.

"Great idea. Shall we go to bed?"

Two

"Whatcha doing?" Jacqui asked her mother, peering over her shoulder at the kitchen table.

"What *are you* doing," Kate corrected, smiling up at her daughter, and then said, "some homework of my own".

"Your work gives you homework?" Jacqui questioned in surprise.

"Not usually. I volunteered to be the first aid officer in our department at work. I thought that because I was on annual leave at the moment, I could get a head start on this reading that I need to do before they give me my first aid certificate."

"What does a first aid officer do?"

"They're the person that you go to if you're unwell or you've hurt yourself. I also need to look out for anything that appears unsafe at work and report on it so that it can be fixed."

"Do you get paid to be a first aid officer?"

"No honey. I volunteered to do it."

"But won't it take up more time at work?"

"If someone needs first aid, yes it will add to what I need to get done in my work hours."

"So why do it?"

"I guess for two reasons. They needed someone to carry out the role at work and by me volunteering to do so; it gives me a current first aid certificate."

"Why would you want one?" Jacqui asked her mother, frowning at the thought.

"Do you remember how I've been working on a website for Genesis?" Kate asked, continuing as her daughter nodded, "I think it'll look even better to potential clients if we're able to say that the owner is up to date on her first aid. That way if any accident were to occur here, I could deal with it safely and parents would feel safer about having their kids here."

Jacqui thought this over, smiling.

"Great idea!"

"You bet," Kate replied with a grin, "much like I don't let you, Geordie and Hannah ride your ponies unless I'm home, I believe some parents would not let their children ride unless someone was around who was trained in first aid."

"So you really did it to benefit Genesis," Jacqui confirmed, going to the fridge to get a glass of juice.

"I did it because I am in a position to do it at work *and* it may benefit our property. Speaking of which, I spoke with Kara yesterday about teaching you girls once a month," Kate continued, referring to the teenage girl who lived next door and who was dating her son.

Jacqui turned her attention back to her mother with an excited grin.

"What did she say?"

"She wanted a little time to think about it. It seemed that she was excited by the idea, but a little nervous too."

"But she's great at teaching! I've learnt so much from her already," Jacqui protested.

"Perhaps you'd like to remind her of that then," Kate replied with a smile.

"What if she says no?" Jacqui asked, looking sad.

Kate smiled.

"Let's give her time to think about it without feeling pressured. Even if Kara isn't sure about teaching you girls each month, I'm sure we'll be able to find someone who is a good horse rider that would be interested in the idea of instructing and helping us set up a riding club on the property. In some ways it may be easier to find an instructor than it will be to make sure we've got a good number of people for them to teach!"

Jacqui nodded, sitting at the kitchen table opposite her mum.

"Well Geordie, Hannah and I would definitely be there each month... and maybe Alice and Megan," Jacqui said, thinking about the two girls who agisted their horses at Genesis.

"And don't forget me."

"You?" Jacqui repeated, incredulous.

Kate laughed.

"Of course! Captain could do with the exercise and I could do with a brush up on my horse riding skills! It only makes sense to me that I would ride with the rest of you lot."

Jacqui frowned suddenly, thinking of Captain's large size and then Magik, the little pony that five year old Megan rode.

"What's wrong?" Kate asked, looking across at her daughter.

"I just thought about the different size in the horses and ponies... plus, you're a lot more experienced than Geordie, Hannah and I, and I think Alice is too. But young Megan has only just gotten the hang of rising to the trot."

Kate smiled.

"That's very true darling. I guess that means that whoever is teaching will have to plan their lessons to suit three different levels of riders. As the riding club grows and we get more agistees, we may be able to have different riding levels and more than one instructor."

Jacqui grinned at the thought.

"That'd be great!"

Kate nodded.

"It would be wonderful. I'd better finish this reading for work. Have you done any of your homework today?"

Jacqui shook her head, rising from the table as she told her mother she would get onto it. She wondered how she was going to do so when she was distracted by the idea of a heap of new agistees and setting up a riding club on their property.

Kate sighed with content, lounging back against the wall of the tie up shed. She was resting on a stack of hay that had been unloaded the day before.

April in Victoria meant the weather was cooling down as autumn headed toward winter. Tony had agreed that getting 100 bales of grass hay was worth investing in, just in case pasture decreased and the horses started dropping in condition. Buying in bulk had meant they were cheaper and Tony had reasoned that they would be able to sell individual bales to their current agistees at a small profit.

It was now Sunday afternoon and the family had finished at church and had lunch. Jacqui and Geordie were out in the house paddock, trying to find suitable areas where they could set up some cross country jumps. Geordie and Hannah had been introduced to the cross country course next door at the East Riding School and were adamant that Genesis needed its own cross country course.

Hannah was due to be dropped off shortly. While Geordie had made a habit of going to church most weeks with the Kings, Jacqui's other close school friend was happy to skip that part of the morning and meet them afterward for some horse related activity or other.

Kate's gaze took in the paddock in front of her where they'd set out a perimeter for an arena. Kate had picked up some arena letters at the local saddlery and spaced these out according to the dimensions of a 60 by 20 metre arena. The three girls plus their other two clients had taken great joy in warming up their ponies in the arena before many a ride out in the paddock.

To Kate's left lay the family home with the house paddock behind that. This was where Geordie and Jacqui were. To her right she could glimpse the start of the driveway that led off the property.

Although she couldn't see them from the tie up shed, Kate knew that the claret ash they'd planted on either side sported deep red leaves at the moment. She was proud to think that her daughter had offered to rake up the leaves once they started to fall. It was lovely how the three girls had taken such delight in making sure the property looked good and was appealing to potential clients.

"Daydreaming again?" a deep male voice questioned, causing Kate to smile down at her husband.

"It's good for my soul," she agreed, her smile widening as he looked for a way up the hay stack.

"Guess it'll probably be good for mine too," Tony replied, stepping carefully before coming to sit beside his wife.

"Where are the girls?"

"In the house paddock planning a cross country course," Kate responded with an amused smile.

Tony's raised eyebrows asked the question before he needed to voice it.

"I guess you weren't around when they came up with that idea," Kate responded, "last week it seems that Geordie and Hannah were introduced to the cross country course at the East Riding School in their lesson. Now all three girls are going to be the next best eventer Australia has seen and they need somewhere to practice!"

Tony laughed.

"They may need some jumps for that, a lot of control and for it to not be approaching typical winter weather."

Kate nodded her agreement, her gaze turning to the driveway as a car pulled up. Quickly Hannah jumped out of the car, looking toward the house.

"Afternoon!" Kate called out, causing the young girl to start in surprise.

"Oh, hi Mrs. King! Are Geordie and Hannah inside?"

"On a day like this?" Kate asked with a smile, "they're in the house paddock planning where the cross country jumps should go."

"Oh!" Hannah said in surprise, turning and running toward the gate behind the house.

Hannah's father laughed, telling the Kings he would be back just after five. The pair nodded and waved as he turned the car around and left.

"Do you think they'll still be in the same paddock at five?" Tony asked knowingly.

Kate smiled, thinking the question hardly required an answer.

"We really should have a few different sized jumps at each spot," Geordie informed Jacqui as they took a photo with Kate's digital camera of another area where they felt a jump could go.

"Why's that?"

"Well at the East, they have three jumps beside each other of different heights. This way the beginners, intermediate and advanced riders can all have a go over the same course, just jumping at different heights," Geordie explained of the riding school where she took fortnightly lessons.

"That's clever!"

"Isn't it?"

"I guess then it means we have to find three different heights of jumps for each area... how do we know what height to have them?"

Geordie shrugged, unsure.

"Hannah will know."

"Know what?" Hannah asked, jogging over to the pair.

Jacqui smiled a hello.

"The different height that jumps should be for different levels of riders... like at the East Riding School."

Hannah nodded.

"I don't know off the top of my head, but if we could get our hands on some jumping or Pony Club books, I'm sure we'd be able to find out."

"Great idea!" Jacqui grinned, thinking how lucky it was she was visiting the library with her mother the following day.

Thinking they'd easily solved that dilemma, the three girls set out to finish taking photos of different areas where they could put jumps before it got dark.

Three

Jacqui focused hard, trying to stay relaxed and balanced as Banjo kept moving at a steady trot around the paddock. The young blonde had told her neighbour Kara about the three girls' plans to set up a cross country course at Genesis.

Kara knew that Jacqui had done a little bit of jumping and took this opportunity to introduce her to a jumping position known as 'two point'. Jacqui had been surprised to learn that she should change how she sat in the saddle coming into a jump and over it.

The idea was that you only had two points of your body in contact with the saddle while you were in jumping position. This was different to the typical three point position that you usually used.

When normally riding a horse and sitting on it correctly, the body comes into contact with the saddle at three different points – the seat of the rider, and the two legs. When riding in two point, the rider lifts their weight out of the saddle so that their seat is no longer touching the saddle.

Jacqui found it very difficult to balance out of the saddle while Kara's older gelding Banjo trotted along. She said as much to Kara.

"It gets easier in the canter, I promise. But just to let you know, it'll get harder first! Banjo is doing a nice slow trot for you, Jacqui. He should actually be moving a lot more forward which would be harder for you. We'll encourage him to trot at a more forward rate when you're a little more used to riding in two point position. You can go back to rising trot now."

Jacqui sighed with relief, allowing her body to rise and fall with the pattern of the gelding's outside front leg.

"This is so much easier!"

Kara nodded in agreement, smiling.

"As you improve at your two point position, it'll make jumping easier on Banjo! The important thing about being a good horse rider is that you're comfortable, but also that your horse is. Banjo can balance better and keep you safer going over a jump if you have a good jumping position, rather than getting thrown about in the saddle."

Jacqui nodded, thinking about this as she brought the gelding back to a walk under Kara's instruction.

"I hadn't thought about making things easier on him. I really am learning so much from you Kara!" Jacqui paused and then continued shyly, glancing at the older teen, "have you thought about instructing at Genesis when we start up a riding club?"

Kara smiled.

"I have… I'm not really sure I'm a good enough rider to be teaching a group of people how to ride their horses better. I have a riding lesson on Prairie next week with my instructor so I thought I'd ask her opinion," she replied, referring to the young grey mare her parents had recently bought her.

"But you're great! I've learnt so many things from you and you explain everything really well," Jacqui protested loudly.

Banjo tossed his head as the young girl tightened the reins unnecessarily.

"I didn't say I wouldn't do it," Kara responded, causing Jacqui to calm down, "and remember you have a large animal under you that responds to your feelings, Jacqui."

Jacqui blushed.

"I'm sorry. Sorry to you too, Banjo," she said, patting the sweet natured horse.

Kara smiled as she walked over to a couple of trot poles she had laid on the ground for Jacqui to practice going over in her two point position.

"I am thinking about it but it feels easy with you Jacqui because you didn't have any expectations at the start. You just wanted to learn about sitting on a horse and we've gone from there. It may be different with other people who have been riding for awhile and maybe even get lessons from somewhere else. They may not like the way I teach or things I suggest they do to improve their riding."

Kara set the two poles up on one tyre each; with the poles crossing over in the middle so that they created a small X shaped jump.

"I guess that's possible," Jacqui reasoned, moving back into a trot under Kara's instruction.

For the next ten minutes the pair worked on Jacqui's jumping position as she moved in a circle around the paddock and over the jump. Kara was insistent that Jacqui look ahead to where she was going. The eleven year old found it very difficult to not look down at the jump! Kara told her repeatedly that where she looked guided the horse and looking down might throw Banjo off balance.

They ended on a good note, but Jacqui knew she'd looked down at the small cross bar jump more often than she'd looked past it. She wondered how she would break that habit as she headed back home across the paddock.

Geordie groaned as the teacher told the class about an assignment they were to work on over the next few weeks.

"But we've only just started back at school!" the lively redhead whispered fervently to Hannah.

Hannah nodded in agreement, frowning as she realised they unintentionally had the teacher's attention.

"Is there a problem girls?" Mrs. Hook asked.

Geordie mumbled 'no', looking down at the sheet that outlined what they needed to do for this project.

"Great. Then I'll continue," their grade six teacher responded cheerfully.

"As I said, we're exploring the idea of endangered and extinct species. I want you to each put together a report on a different animal that includes where it can be found in the world, how many are left and why it appears to be suffering the threat of extinction. Any information that you find about how this can be stopped should be included, as

17

well as a description on what the animal looks like. Yes, Jacqui?" Mrs. Hook asked, noting her raised hand.

"Would it be ok if we chose an animal that was already extinct but treated it as if it were still on the endangered list?"

Mrs. Hook smiled, considering the idea.

"I'll allow it as long as you can answer each of the questions on this project sheet. I'd also like all of you to tell me by Friday which animal you've chosen."

There was a loud groan from the majority of the class. Their teacher laughed at the protest.

"There is logic behind my request. Many of you leave things to the last minute and don't know where to start. If you tell me what animal you've chosen, that gets the hard part out of the way."

Jacqui smiled at their teacher's reasoning. She missed Mr. O'Laughlin whom they'd had as their grade five teacher last year, but Mrs. Hook, although she was stricter with the students, didn't appear to be mean.

The young girl was rapt to find that she could choose an extinct animal instead. When she'd visited the library the other week with her mother to seek out some pony club books, she'd also found a large book of horse breeds listed alphabetically.

An animal named the Quagga had been under the letter Q. Apparently it was an extinct breed of the Equus family with some unusual stripes across its head and neck, but not across its body. Jacqui had thought at the time that it looked a little bit like a zebra. She was excited to think that

18

she could now focus on a horse breed for their grade six endangered species assignment.

Geordie nudged Jacqui in the side.

"Why do you look so excited?" she asked her friend suspiciously, glancing up at Mrs. Hook to make sure her attention was elsewhere.

The teacher was compiling a list of student names and chosen animal from those who had already decided. Jacqui giggled.

"Because I was reading about an extinct breed of horse last week and I still have the book at home. I think half of the answers I need for this project are already in that book."

Geordie raised her brows in surprise.

"No fair! Do you know of another breed of horse I could do out of that book?"

Jacqui shook her head, indicating that she didn't.

"Sorry."

Geordie sighed.

"Oh well, I guess I'll have to do the Tasmanian Devil or something like that."

Their teacher came around to the girl's table, asking if they'd already decided on a species to do the project on. Jacqui hurriedly mentioned the Quagga, keen to have it on record that she was doing the horse breed. Mrs. Hook smiled.

"I wondered if you had a horse breed in mind for this assignment when you asked about an extinct species," she responded, turning her attention to Hannah next.

"And what about you, Hannah?"

"I'd love to do the Prez... walskis Horse," she replied, causing Geordie to look at her in surprise.

"Zevalski's Horse I think is how it's pronounced," Mrs. Hook responded as she wrote this down beside Hannah's name.

The table of five girls looked at their teacher in surprise. When she looked back up at them she couldn't help but laugh.

"You're not the only people interested in horses!" she replied with a grin, causing a few of the girls to laugh in delight.

"Now what about you, Geordie?"

Geordie sighed.

"You wouldn't happen to know another breed of horse that is endangered or extinct, would you, Mrs. Hook?" she asked hopefully.

Their teacher smiled.

"I'm afraid not. However, you can take the time to look into it and get back to me. Or maybe you could think a little bit outside of the box," she responded cryptically.

Geordie frowned.

"What do you mean?"

"Well what if there was a type of seahorse that was endangered? Or maybe even a hippopotamus, which is known as the water horse? However, you may have to move past the *equus* family and find something else entirely."

Geordie agreed that she would think a while longer before making a decision. She was pleasantly surprised by their teacher's other suggestions. She hadn't even considered a seahorse!

Mrs. Hook checked with Caitlin and Amelia if they'd decided on a species of animal before moving onto the next table.

"Do you think we should all get together and start on this assignment once we've made our choice?" Hannah suggested, gaining a nod from Amelia and Caitlin.

"What if we do it even before Geordie's decided?" Jacqui suggested, wanting to get started right away.

"Maybe we can help you find something horse related to do your project on while we work on ours," she directed to Geordie.

The young redhead smiled.

"That'd be great! Then I won't feel like I'm the only one who hasn't been able to start on their assignment because they didn't make a choice."

The five girls agreed that they'd stay back at the library on Wednesday afternoon after school, as was their normal habit with homework. Jacqui thought she'd check with her mum about the group meeting up at Genesis on Friday, too. She was keen to learn more about the Quagga and to get the project finished so she could spend more time riding Matty.

Four

Kate sighed and wiped her gloved hands across her jeans. She was glad to have thrown the last biscuit of hay out into the paddock for the horses and ponies on the property. A light drizzle of rain was gathering drops around the rim of her Akubra hat. The weather was particularly cold.

Tony had done a great job of convincing their four current agistees that it'd be worth each purchasing a couple of bales of hay to keep their horse's roughage level up. There had been a week of consistent rains which although great for the pastures, had resulted in high water content in the grass. The horses could eat all day and take in a lot of water, which didn't help to keep their weight – or keep them warm.

Kate had reasoned that if their clients were willing to pay for the hay at the rate they'd set, she would make sure each animal got one biscuit morning and night. Most had agreed to this, with young Alice saying she'd be happy to feed Sox and Magik on the weekends.

Kate sent up a silent prayer of thanks as she heard the rumble of a car coming down the driveway. An older gentleman had called earlier in the week seeking somewhere cheap to agist his three mares. He indicated that they were actually for sale but until he'd found new homes for them, he was keen to find somewhere a little cheaper than the current place he was at.

With the cold weather and rain, Kate hadn't been sure if he'd come out that afternoon as planned. She was relieved she was wrong. Even if he was to be a short term client, the idea of three more horses on the property was extremely appealing. Perhaps the new purchasers would be happy to keep their horses at Genesis too. That would be a real answer to prayer.

Kate grinned as some sun broke through the clouds and the rain seemed to cease.

"Your timing really is wonderful," she murmured to her Creator, turning her attention to the vehicle that had pulled up beside her.

The driver wound down the windows and called out the passenger side to Kate.

"They sure look happy for that hay! I'm looking for the property owner, Kate?"

Kate smiled, thinking if only she and Tony did own Genesis.

"I'm Kate," she replied as she took off her gloves.

"Wonderful!" the older gentleman responded, putting the car into park and exiting the vehicle.

"I'm Bob," he responded, offering his hand to her to shake.

"I wasn't sure if this weather would put you off coming out to check out the property," Kate admitted, leaning against the wheelbarrow with a half bale of hay still in it.

"Little bit of rain never hurt anyone!" Bob replied, pausing with a smile, "paying more than you need to for agistment on the other hand…"

Kate smiled.

"Can I show you around?" she offered.

Bob agreed and for the next twenty minutes the pair took a look at the facilities Genesis had to offer. Bob also took in a brief view of each paddock. He was impressed that the horses were confined to two of the five paddocks on offer while the King's worked to eradicate as many weeds as possible from the other paddocks. Bob said as much to Kate.

"We would love to subdivide the paddocks in the future so that there is more chance to rotate and manage pastures," Kate confided, "but at least for now with the size they are, we know they can hold a decent number of horses. The two ponies in the driveway paddock are kept separately for their owners who are willing to pay a little more for this."

Bob nodded his head, taking in the whole property once again.

"Well I'm happy for my three girls to go out with the other horses and see how they go. I'm rapt to find that you have an area where I'll be able to work the girls to get them back into shape for sale."

"So you'll ride the three mares yourself?" Kate asked, thinking that if she could still be riding at Bob's age, she would be happy.

"Of course! I may be seventy but I still ride better than many I know," he responded proudly, walking with Kate back towards his car.

Kate laughed.

"I didn't mean to imply otherwise. Well Bob, if you're happy to have your girls here we can put them out in the freeway paddock with the others. But first I'd like to contain them in the smaller paddock behind our tie up area. If I can observe them for a couple of weeks and see that they're healthy, then I'll be only too happy to introduce them to sharing a paddock with the other horses."

"Good woman, I like your thinking. When would you like me to bring them by?" Bob questioned, causing Kate to smile in relief.

"Whenever suits you, Bob. There are only a couple of days left in April and we charge monthly, so if you're happy to pay for May up front, we'll waive the last few days of April."

"Deal!" Bob replied, shaking her hand.

Bob indicated that he had a float to travel the three mares over and asked if he could store it on the property. Kate didn't see why not and pointed out a grassy area near to where Bob had pulled up that he could back the float into. As the older man headed back down the driveway, Kate sent another prayer of thanks to God.

"What time is dad coming home?" Jacqui asked, cutting up the lamb chops her mother had made.

"Sometime after seven," Kate responded with a concerned frown.

Tony had rung at five to indicate he would be late. Jody, his manager, had insisted that the team stay back and fix a problem that had become evident that day, before the following morning's meeting.

Tony hadn't seen a way around it and pointed out to Kate that it was a one off occurrence that did need to be fixed that day. Kate had said she'd keep dinner warm for him.

"I want to tell him all about the Quagga," Jacqui continued, not noting her mother's concern, "I found lots in that book I borrowed but there's even more online."

"Did Geordie find an animal to do her report on?" Ross asked, having heard of nothing but their project for the last five days.

Jacqui grinned, saying that she had.

"So... what did she choose?" Ross questioned, causing Kate to smile.

"Oh! A particular type of seahorse. I forget what it's called... Ross, did you talk to Kara about teaching all of us at the Genesis riding club?" Jacqui asked, her attention moving elsewhere.

Ross rolled his eyes.

"I can't get away from horses in this household and then you want me to talk about them with my girlfriend too!" he responded shortly.

Jacqui smiled.

"At least you know it's a topic she likes," she counteracted.

Kate laughed. Ross sighed, admitting that was true.

"I did," he conceded, causing Jacqui to grin in triumph.

"And?" she questioned, eagerly awaiting the response.

Kate smiled at how quickly the tables had turned in her children's conversation.

"She said she'd talked with her riding instructor and that he'd encouraged her to do it. Apparently he said that teaching others can help to improve your own understanding of something, so he told Kara to give it a go."

"Yes!" Jacqui responded in triumph, "I wasn't sure she would do it... I hadn't realised her instructor was a male."

Ross frowned.

"Yeah... she got a new one a few riding lessons back. Now all I hear about is 'Jack says this, Jack says that.' It's a bit much to hear so often."

Jacqui shrugged and told her brother that if he was helping to improve Kara's riding, then that was the main thing. She turned her attention back to her dinner. Kate watched her son carefully, wondering if he was feeling a bit jealous.

She made a note to ask Ross about it when he was alone. Feeling her gaze, Ross looked up from his meal.

"What?" he asked defensively.

Kate smiled and continued with her own meal.

"Nothing honey. How did soccer go this afternoon?"

Finding this topic to be more to his liking, Ross cheered up and gave Kate a run down of the practice match they'd had that afternoon. They were playing against another local team that Saturday. Kate was glad to find that her son was looking forward to the game. She was going to miss it unfortunately so that she could keep an eye on the girls riding at Genesis. Tony would take him and watch the game. Kate would have to settle with a run down from her son later that day.

Five

Kate smiled as she watched Jacqui, Geordie and Hannah trotting around the property arena Saturday afternoon. The 60 metre by 20 metre riding area was little more than a flat section in a paddock, lined by railway sleepers. It was simple but served its purpose effectively.

A young gentleman Jacob Smith was hired by the Kings to carry out odd jobs a few hours each week. He would soon be putting in a railing around the arena to help with future plans of riding lessons being conducted in it. Geordie and Hannah were thrilled to be helping – the two girls volunteered at Genesis in return for agistment for their ponies.

Kate had ridden her gelding Captain earlier with the three girls but after three quarters of an hour had decided the older horse had had enough. He was now unsaddled, brushed and munching on some hay in the tie up area. Kate had insisted the girls have a short break to have something to eat and drink in the cooler weather before going back out on their ponies. It was the insistence that their ponies couldn't be expected to exercise all day without a break that had caused the girls to agree.

Now they were warming the three ponies up again before heading out to the house paddock for a game of follow the leader.

As Kate glanced over the three girls, she noted how much Jacqui had grown over the past few months. The young blonde appeared to be going through a growth spurt. She would soon be taller than Hannah and had already overtaken Geordie in height.

Kate didn't like to mention it just yet, but she felt her daughter would soon outgrow the little bay pony, Matty. His lease was renewed and paid for each month but Kate wasn't sure they would need to do so for much longer. She also wasn't sure Jacqui would welcome this news. For now it could wait.

A horse snorted nearby and Kate turned with a smile to the farm's quarantine paddock. It now housed Bob's three grey mares. They'd arrived Friday afternoon, along with Bob providing a month's worth of agistment for each mare.

Kate finished earlier on a Friday and had been secretly pleased that the banks were still open when Bob had seen his girls settled and headed off for the day. Whilst leasing Genesis, Tony and Kate were working hard to secure some savings that they could use in the future to buy a property.

As far as the mother of two was concerned, the sooner she could put any extra funds into their savings account, the sooner the money could get to work earning interest. They had a nice sum forming but she knew it was still far from a decent deposit for a block of land.

Noting that Captain had finished his hay, she untied the gelding and headed toward the freeway paddock to put him back out. The three girls headed in the other direction, warmed up for their game of follow the leader.

"You didn't signal that you were going to slow down!" Hannah complained to Geordie, having almost run into the back of her.

Jacqui was glad that Matty had been cantering more slowly than the other two and came back to a walk easily. The little bay pony was very responsive to his rider's seat and aids. Jacqui nodded in agreement, causing Geordie to blush.

"Sorry! I know I should have let you both know. I was just thinking and got distracted and I guess Rose felt that. She was actually the one who stopped suddenly – I thought I might fall off!"

Jacqui giggled.

"They really are sensitive, aren't they?" she stated in wonder.

The three continued on at a walk side by side. Jacqui told them about her lesson with Kara earlier in the week and getting upset whilst riding Banjo.

"Kara told me off for getting Banjo worked up," she confided in her two friends.

"That's not very nice!" Geordie responded hotly.

"Well, she reminded me that my feelings are communicated to the horse I ride. It felt like she was telling me off, but I think it was necessary to remind me that I can't forget about the horse I'm riding."

Hannah nodded her head in agreement.

"Emmy often tells us that at the East Riding School. Jack does too, if he takes us for a lesson," she informed Jacqui.

"Jack?" Jacqui questioned, not having heard of another instructor at the riding school.

"Yeah. He tends to take more of the jumping classes and the more experienced riders but we've had him a couple of times."

"Kara recently got a new riding instructor called Jack… could it be the same man?" Jacqui questioned, unsure.

Geordie shrugged her shoulders. Hannah pondered the question for a few seconds.

"I would guess so. Emmy mentioned that he has clients outside of the East Riding School, so why not Kara?"

"So… if we needed more instructors for Genesis, we could maybe hire him or Emmy?" Jacqui questioned with a grin.

"Great idea!" Geordie enthused.

Hannah frowned.

"I'm not so sure… I don't think Emmy teaches away from her parents' riding school. And I think it is cheaper to get a lesson with Jack at the East than it is to have him come out to where you have your horse."

"But maybe the East Riding School is cheaper with Jack because it's a group lesson? If we had a group of riders here at Genesis maybe it would cost us less to hire an instructor," Jacqui suggested, her two friends shrugging their shoulders.

"Perhaps we can ask when we next have a riding lesson," Geordie suggested, causing Jacqui to smile.

"That'd be great!"

"But we'd also need a group of people here riding at Genesis to make it worthwhile for another instructor to come and teach…" Hannah reminded the girls.

"True," Jacqui sighed, the three riding on in silence.

As they rode past the first point where a cross country jump was to be put in, Geordie changed the subject.

"So when do you think Genesis will have a cross country course?" she asked Jacqui.

Jacqui shrugged, surprised to think she'd forgotten about all the plans they'd made.

"You know, I don't know! I know we talked with mum about it after we worked out where each jump should go… then school started back and I got caught up with learning about the Quagga. How is your report going, Geordie?" she asked the fiery redhead.

Geordie sighed.

"Ok, I guess. I've found a couple of good websites but they seem to have the same information repeated. But they disagree on how many are left in the world. I don't know which number to use."

"Perhaps you need to show that information to Mrs. Hook and see what she thinks," Hannah suggested, gaining a nod from her friend.

"That's a good idea! At least then she'll know I'm researching my topic, I just don't know which information to believe."

Jacqui nodded, agreeing that was probably Geordie's best option.

"I wonder how Amelia and Caitlin are going with their reports," she said suddenly, thinking of their other two close friends.

"Oh they've both finished!" Hannah responded, causing Jacqui to look at her in surprise.

Jacqui frowned as she felt annoyed at this answer. She was surprised to find that she liked to be the first one to finish their reports and feel like she was ahead in school.

"That was quick!" she replied, causing Hannah to smile.

"Yeah… they both got asked out last week by Adam and Jordan on a double date. Apparently their parents agreed they could go to a movie this weekend only if they'd finished all of their outstanding homework."

Geordie snorted in disdain at this piece of news. Jacqui continued riding along quietly, thoughtful.

"I'd rather have Rose as my incentive to get schoolwork finished on time. Boys can be so silly!" she burst out strongly.

Hannah shrugged, not ready to agree with her friend.

"What do you think, Jacqui?"

Jacqui looked across to Hannah.

"I'm not sure… if Caitlin and Amelia want to go out with Adam and Jordan, I think it's fair enough that their parents make sure school work is done… like we have to before we get to spend time with our horses. I just think that girls are easier to talk to than boys," she commented shyly.

"And horses are even easier to talk to!" Geordie responded with glee, pushing Rose into a steady trot.

Hannah was quick to ask Jasper to trot and before too long had pushed him into a canter, calling back to the others, "last one back to the tie up area is a rotten egg!"

Jacqui grinned, asking Matty to run after the other two. Horses were indeed easier to talk to!

Six

Jacqui watched the older gentleman Bob put his saddle onto one of his grey mares. She frowned as she took in the frame of the saddle, thinking it looked very different to what she and the other girls rode in. She said as much to Bob.

"This here is a dressage saddle," he responded, making sure the saddle blanket was evenly on the mare's back before he put the saddle on top.

"Venetian likes it when I work her in a dressage saddle," he continued, speaking of the mare.

"All of your mares have names that start with V. Is that your favourite letter?" Jacqui asked curiously, holding her hand out for Venetian to sniff.

Bob laughed. It was a hearty sound. He moved back around from the right hand side of the mare after checking the girth wasn't twisted.

"I think I should choose a better favourite letter for naming horses! My three girls are warmblood mares. It is tradition to name them something that starts with the same letter as their father's name. Unfortunately for me, his name is Volksraad!"

Jacqui grinned at the new piece of information.

"I wonder if Matty is named in that way," she questioned out loud.

"You never know! I doubt it though, only us silly warmblood people set a rule like that," Bob replied with a wink as he tightened the girth.

Jacqui returned his smile.

"Can I watch you work Venetian, Bob?" she asked, curious to see what made dressage so different to her riding with Geordie and Hannah.

"Of course! It is your property that I'm riding on, after all," the older gentleman replied.

My property. Jacqui thought that sounded delightful. She followed Bob out toward the arena, being careful to walk beside him rather than behind the large mare. Bob had quickly instructed her about the safest place to walk – even if she was shy about walking beside someone else's horse, it was much safer than walking along behind where the horse may not see or hear her.

Kate came out to join her daughter as Bob warmed his mare up.

"Did you know that warmblood horses are named by the same letter as their father's name?" Jacqui asked her mother, proud of her new found fact.

"I didn't! It sounds like you've been learning a bit from Bob," Kate replied with a smile.

Jacqui beamed.

"I have! He was telling me about his dressage saddle. Have you done dressage before, mum?"

"I have, Jacqui. Dressage is a form of educating a horse that you may know as flat work. When you warm up Matty with the other girls and you make sure he is responding to what you ask, this is a form of dressage. In its most advanced form, the horse looks very graceful and sometimes it's hard to tell that the rider is asking anything of the horse. It looks beautiful. Maybe we'll get to see some of these advanced moves as Bob is riding Venetian."

The pair stood at the side of the arena and watched as Bob put Venetian into a steady trot. The older man sat deeply in the saddle, not rising at all.

"I don't think I look that neat when I do the sitting trot!" Jacqui exclaimed.

Kate smiled.

"You'll improve the more you try it honey. But it's good for you to keep practising your rising trot, too. I'm sure Matty feels more balanced when you do."

Jacqui nodded. She watched Bob quietly, listening intently as her mother explained certain things the older man was doing or asking his mare to do. Jacqui concluded that it was very interesting watching dressage, but even more fun to be riding herself!

Saturday afternoon Jacqui had another riding lesson with Kara. She excitedly told the teenager about Bob and his three grey mares. Kara listened with interest.

"I'd love to see them! I enjoy my jumping but prefer dressage. I'd be curious to see how he rides his warmbloods."

"Perhaps you could ask Ross about coming over to see them," Jacqui suggested as she picked up a trot, rising to the left diagonal as instructed by Kara.

"I could," Kara agreed, "but I think Ross hears enough about horses! I doubt he'd want me visiting him and then using all of the time to talk horses with someone else."

Jacqui thought about this as she rode along, cutting across in front of Kara and sitting for three beats of the trot to change her diagonal. She then changed the direction of her trotting circle to help warm up Banjo.

"Maybe... I could invite you over one afternoon instead?" she offered shyly, "Bob seems to work one of his mares each afternoon, sometimes two..."

Kara grinned at the suggestion.

"That sounds great, Jacqui! If you check with Bob and tell me when you're happy to have a guest, I'd love to come by and visit."

Jacqui grinned. She hadn't been sure that the older girl would be interested in spending any time with her outside of teaching her about being a better rider. She was pleasantly surprised to find that Kara was eager to do so.

That afternoon the pair worked on Jacqui's focus over jumps again. Kara stood in line with the small jump Jacqui was to go over and held up her hand. Jacqui needed to call out the number of fingers Kara held up quickly as Jacqui went over the jump.

With Jacqui so focused on not missing the number of fingers, she was looking beyond the jump, rather than down at it. She grinned with excitement at how easy it now seemed to not look at the jump. She said as much to Kara.

"That was a great idea of yours!" she confided in her friend, letting Banjo walk on a loose rein as he cooled down.

"Thanks! But I've got to admit it wasn't my idea. My new instructor Jack suggested it to me when I asked his advice in my last lesson. Apparently his girlfriend uses it to teach riders that are first learning to jump."

"Well it's still a great idea," Jacqui responded, patting Banjo on the neck as she thought about what a good lesson they'd had.

The girls parted ways with Jacqui promising to check with Bob about watching him ride. Kara seemed as excited about the idea as Jacqui was. Thinking about this as she raced across the paddock, Jacqui suddenly wondered how Ross' soccer match had gone. She couldn't wait to tell him that Kara was coming over the following week to spend some time with her!

Seven

Jacqui lay in bed a couple of weeks later, thanking God for the wonderful day she'd had. Kara had made a few trips to visit with her and watch Bob ride his mares. The young teen had been amazed to see how well the older gentleman rode. She had amused him with all of her questions.

Bob had been only too happy to answer her. He commented that the better he could explain something to help someone else understand; the better understanding it helped him to have of horse riding. This had only cemented Jack's encouragement to Kara to take up instructing of lower level riders.

Jacqui had been thrilled that conversation quickly turned to the idea of a riding club at Genesis. Before she knew it, Bob and Kara had decided to each teach at Genesis the following Saturday – *if* there were students to teach! Jacqui had waited impatiently to be able to talk this over with her mother, and Geordie and Hannah of course!

That was what had occurred today – Genesis had held its first riding club day. The younger three riders had two lessons in the morning, with Kara instructing them on the flat and then over jumps. They'd had an absolute ball in both sessions. Jacqui hoped that Alice would be able to join them the following month when the next session was planned.

After lunch, Kara and Kate had had a lesson with Bob instructing them. Geordie, Hannah and Jacqui had taken great delight in watching the older riders ride. Geordie had giggled the first time Bob gruffly told Kate to stop flopping around on her horse's back at the sitting trot!

After the horses had been cooled down, all six of them sat down for a theory lesson. Bob had provided some history on the warmblood breed the Hanoverian and then Kate had taught the girls about vital signs of the horse and what was considered normal.

Both Geordie and Hannah had commented on how successful the day was. Hannah indicated that the riding was great, but she also learnt so much watching others ride and in the theory lesson. Jacqui and Geordie had been of the same opinion and it was with unanimous agreement by the six attendees that they would repeat the session each month.

Being run on a Saturday, it hadn't interfered with church and Ross and Tony were again out for Ross' soccer match. His team had won the fortnight before and had a draw on the day of the riding club. Jacqui was excited to think that Kara was able to dedicate one Saturday a month to coming to Genesis to teach and ride, and that Ross wasn't jealous of his girlfriend's time because he was focused on his favourite sport. It all seemed to have fit together perfectly.

Kate grinned as she proudly watched Jacqui leading Matty around the round yard, young James Smith sitting tall on his back, with a large grin. The Smith family had come over for lunch again after church.

Cindy Smith was looking very heavily pregnant on account of it being mid-May. She was only too happy to accept a seat offered to her by Kate. From her position she could see James being taught to ride and keep an eye on the other two eagerly awaiting their turn outside the round yard. Jacqui had insisted they could watch at the gate but that the pair needed to stand back a little for safety reasons. They'd dutifully obeyed the older girl, not wanting to miss out on an opportunity to ride Matty.

Jacob had proudly shown his wife the works he'd been carrying out on the farm each week. When Tony and Kate had approached the pair about Jacob working a set number of hours each week, they'd readily accepted the offer.

Kate felt it was such a small contribution to an income that needed to support a family that would very shortly be six members. She had to remind herself that it wasn't her job to provide for the Smiths, however, it was God's. She was glad that they could offer a small proportion of reliable income, and friendship of course.

"Are you comfortable enough?" Kate asked.

Her gaze was on Jacqui but her question was directed to Cindy.

"Thank you! It's such a relief to be off my feet and to know that my husband is occupied, and the three kids are safely entertained with Jacqui. I must admit, I look forward to church each week when I know I can just sit for an hour or so without having to worry about doing something for the family," Cindy confided softly.

Kate looked at the younger mum and smiled.

"I think that's understandable! I really don't think men appreciate how much work it can be to be a mother! And here you are Cindy, raising three kids whilst growing a fourth!"

Cindy blushed at the compliment.

"It is increasingly tiring, especially with me being pregnant. I can't wait to meet this fourth little one and yet I know it'll mean many sleepless nights. How do you find working and raising children?"

"I think it's a little easier for me! I work part time and Ross and Jacqui are in school five days a week. As long as I'm home when they are and I know that I have weekends with my family, I'm happy. It just helps us financially for me to be earning an income, too."

Cindy nodded, commenting that she looked forward to when she could help Jacob contribute to supporting the children. Kate smiled, saying that she already was.

"How so?" Cindy asked, confused.

"I know Jacob is earning the income currently, but you're helping to contribute to the household through the food that you grow at home, the support and nourishment you provide to your children and through having a meal on the table for your husband when he gets home. That's just as important!"

Cindy sat quietly, thinking this over. Kate let her ponder the statement as she watched Jacqui lift James off her little bay pony and put one of the other Smith children on.

The first time the Smiths had visited, Kate had sent them home with a bucket full of home grown vegetables.

Cindy had been hesitant to accept the offer but when the two families next caught up at church, she'd asked Kate to direct her on plants that could easily be grown in their small yard. Kate had been only too delighted to research this information for Cindy and gift her with some packets of seed.

Now the young mother was harvesting some of her own vegetables. The Smith and King mothers had even gotten into a habit of bartering with each other – when they had too much of something, they swapped for another vegetable the other had grown. It was working out well for both families.

Kate recognised in both Cindy and Jacob a willingness to learn how to be better stewards with what they were given. They were also eagerly learning about God and the bible, something for which Kate was very thankful. She and Tony prayed for the young couple often and helped them in any way they could.

An hour later all three children had had a couple of short rides on Matty, each finishing up with a little trot. James had laughed with delight, while four year old Tim looked a little afraid. Kate and Cindy had laughed in wonder when three year old Chloe had sat astride Matty, looking like royalty. She bounced along calmly when Jacqui asked Matty to trot and waved happily to her mother when they came back to a walk.

Kate and Jacqui took great delight in relaying this information to Tony later that evening. Ross was busy chatting on the phone with Kara.

As it hit nine o'clock Kate reminded their daughter that she should be getting ready for bed. With a yawn Jacqui nodded, saying goodnight to her parents before going off to brush her teeth.

"What time are you starting tomorrow?" Kate asked, turning her attention to her husband.

Tony sighed.

"I've decided to head in an hour early. Jody has become very demanding each Monday morning – I don't know what must get into her over the weekend! Maybe she goes home and can't switch off from work and develops a list of things she'd like to achieve over the next week..." Tony mused.

"Anyway," he continued after a pause, "as soon as she's in the office, anything I have planned goes out the window. It seems that her requests must be carried out immediately. Not wanting to be disrespectful, I find that I put aside tasks that appear more pressing because she's asked me to do something else. If I can get in and work out what I need to do for the week, then I can prioritise. Then I won't feel that I've only achieved what she's asked of me, not what the company expects of me."

Kate nodded, frowning.

"She does sound like a difficult manager. How are the other staff members responding to her?"

Tony thought this over, stretching out on the couch.

"Not so well. A couple have already had terse words with her and Nick appears really stressed. He does what she asks but seems to be struggling with the working environment. Things feel a lot tenser than before she took on this role."

"Has Clarkeson noticed?" Kate asked, referring to the manager above Jody.

Tony shook his head.

"I don't think so. He pokes his head in on a Tuesday morning every few weeks to see how everyone in the office is. We're all madly trying to get done what's been requested of us that I think it probably appears as if we're all just working hard and very focused. I have wondered a couple of times if I should speak with him... but what would I say?"

Kate sat silently for awhile, thinking.

"That seems a difficult position to be in. We can pray for your workmates and you – that things will become easier, communication will be good with Jody and that you'll manage the stress well. I'm not sure how I'd respond if I found out my staff were speaking against my management ways to someone above me."

Tony nodded, agreeing.

"I think that's what's holding me back from going to Clarkeson. I'm coping ok, but I'm not impressed about working earlier or later than I get paid for. I worry about how the other three are coping though."

Kate nodded.

"That's understandable honey," she paused to listen for sounds in the kitchen, "it sounds like Ross is off the phone. Will we call it a night? We can pray over your work situation before we go to bed."

Tony nodded, thinking this a good idea. The pair got ready for bed before speaking with their God about Tony's work concerns, their desires for their children, their marriage and the wellbeing of the Smith family. Kate thanked God as her eyes closed that her working environment appeared a lot less stressful than her husband's. She was thankful too that she could carry out some study alongside work and raising a family.

Eight

Jacqui frowned as she thought about the riding lesson she'd just had. She was walking back across the freeway paddock of Genesis, towards the house.

Kara had dissolved into a fit of giggles the third time Jacqui had tried to go over a small cross bar jump. Although she and Matty went over it, each time they had knocked one of the rails down. Jacqui had thought it was something she was doing and tried to stay focused, looking beyond the jump to where she wanted to go after she landed.

She'd been very surprised – and a little hurt – to have the older girl laughing at her riding. When she'd asked Kara what she'd done wrong, this caused a further fit of giggles.

"You're actually riding it really well, Jacqui. Matty is being pointed toward the middle of the jump and he's listening to you. The reason the jump is coming down is because your long legs are knocking one of the rails! I think you're getting too big for your pony!" she'd replied, amused at this dilemma.

Jacqui was far from amused. The idea that she would outgrow Matty had never occurred to her. And not this soon! She had concluded that Kara must be wrong and it was something to do with the way she rode over the jump

49

that was the issue. She pondered this as she walked in the front door, leaving her riding boots on the shoe rack.

"Mum, I'm back!" she called out, hanging her jacket up.

It was getting quite cold outside but Jacqui couldn't imagine not riding. She and Kate had gone shopping for a rug for Matty earlier in the month. This had been a whole new learning experience for Jacqui as she was taught by her mother how to find a rug of the right size and then how to put it on in a safe manner. *There was so much to learn about horses!*

When Jacqui had proudly shown off Matty's rug to Geordie and Hannah, the pair had decided they must ask their parents if they could get rugs for Jasper and Rose. Jacqui had been excited to do something before the other two considered it.

"How did your ride go?" Kate called out from the kitchen, interrupting Jacqui's thoughts.

"Ok," Jacqui responded, heading into the kitchen to get a warm drink.

"Just ok?" Kate asked in surprise as Jacqui topped up the kettle and flicked the on switch.

"I couldn't seem to get things right going over the jump today," Jacqui responded, spooning some sugar and cocoa into a mug.

She sat down at the table after she'd poured her drink, thinking. Kate watched her daughter curiously, cutting up some pumpkin for dinner.

"Mum, do you think I could hurt Matty?" Jacqui asked, causing her mother to pause in surprise.

"Not intentionally, Jacqui. Why would you ask such a thing?"

"Kara thinks I'm getting too big for him. Does that mean I'll hurt him?"

Understanding dawned on Kate and she smiled.

"You have had a growth spurt, darling. Remember we had to go shopping for some new school shorts and pants recently."

Jacqui nodded, not happy with the answer her mother had given her.

"So I'm hurting him?"

Kate shook her head.

"I don't think so. You're quite light in build Jacqui. I think you'll find that you're going to get too tall for little Matty, not too heavy. Did Kara say that your riding was upsetting him?"

Jacqui thought about this. She remembered Kara saying that she was riding Matty well. She shook her head.

"I don't think so... Kara was laughing today because she thought my legs were knocking down the jump."

Kate fought back a smile.

"I think Matty would let you know if he was in pain or uncomfortable. Does he seem to be less responsive to you?"

Jacqui shook her head again, indicating that he wasn't.

"Well I think Matty would be the first one to let you know if he was getting hurt. You're the first to know if you

51

feel unwell, aren't you? Sometimes you have to tell me because I don't notice."

Jacqui thought about this, a small smile making its way to her face.

"Yeah. I guess if he was sore he'd be behaving differently. So I can keep riding him?"

"I think so Jacqui. I guess there will come a time when you find that your size will make it difficult to do certain things if you continue to ride Matty. Then you may want to think about using a bigger horse."

Jacqui frowned.

"Who?"

"Well there is Captain," Kate offered, not thinking of any other alternatives for the time being.

"But he's yours, mum!"

"Captain belongs to the family," Kate corrected her daughter.

"But would we both be able to ride him each month at the club?"

Kate considered this for a moment.

"I think he'd cope ok with that. You ride Matty more often than I ride Captain. If and when the time came that you needed a bigger horse, I think Captain would be up to being exercised more often. We'd just have to share him and make sure he gets time off each week – you do that with Matty now. If Matty can handle being ridden in two different lessons at our riding club, I'm sure three lessons wouldn't be too much to ask of Captain."

"Well I hope we don't have to ask that of Captain anytime soon!" Jacqui responded honestly, rising from the table with her cup of cocoa.

"I'm going to get changed before dinner," she told her mum, heading down the hallway.

Kate grinned, glad that her daughter seemed a little happier since coming in the door. It was true that Jacqui seemed to be growing quite a bit. Hopefully this would pause so she could enjoy her responsive little bay pony awhile longer. Kate prayed that this would be the case.

\---

"Hey, who are they?" Geordie asked of her two friends, looking toward the Genesis driveway.

"Who?" Jacqui asked, glancing up to where Geordie was pointing.

The young blonde frowned, not thinking they were expecting any more agistees. At least, her mother hadn't said so. She shrugged helplessly at Geordie.

"I'm not sure. It's great if we've got more people to agist their horses here… but it'd be better if they weren't turning up just before our riding club starts!" she replied, causing Geordie to nod her head in agreement.

"Maybe that's the point," Hannah responded with a smile, causing both of her friends to frown.

"What's the point?" Geordie asked, returning to brushing down Rose.

"Maybe they're turning up for the riding club."

"Can they do that?" Jacqui asked, causing Hannah to laugh.

"I think you'd know that answer better than me – it is your parents' property!" she replied.

Jacqui continued to brush Matty but kept an eye on the cars that made their way into the arena paddock and then continued toward them at a slow pace. She was surprised to find that there were two vehicles, each pulling a float. Trotting bareback behind them was Alice on Sox.

"Hey, here comes Alice!" Jacqui said with a smile, starting to put the saddle on Matty.

Alice had said that her younger sister wasn't yet up to the riding club but that she'd love to check it out. Apparently she attended a local Pony Club one Sunday a month, but was happy to try out one that ran on a Saturday. She'd suggested to Jacqui that maybe she could do both!

Kate came over to see how the girls were going with getting ready. Before they rode in their lesson with Kara, they needed to have Kate check that their saddles and bridles were on correctly.

"Mum, do we have new agistees?" Jacqui asked, doing up the throatlatch strap on Matty's bridle.

"Unfortunately not honey. Alice spoke with me about attending the riding club and mentioned she had a couple of girlfriends from her Pony Club that would also be interested. She asked if it'd be ok if they came along to check things out. I spoke with both of the girls last night about their horse riding and their horses' health and decided it would be ok if they came and joined us today. Kara seemed happy to have a few more people to instruct as it seems they ride at a similar level to Alice."

"Oh!" Jacqui replied, surprised she hadn't known sooner, "well that's great, I guess. It'll sure be different riding with three other people, two that we don't know."

"That's true. But it'll also give you each someone else to learn from. And it'll be a good chance for Kara to gain some more teaching experience. I'd better direct the girls towards where they can get their horses ready," Kate commented suddenly, turning toward the two floats that had just pulled up beside where the girls were getting their ponies ready.

Already tacked up, Geordie watched curiously.

"Hey, what a nice looking roan!" she stated appreciatively, watching the red and white haired horse that was backed out of the first float.

"Isn't he gorgeous? That's Bentleigh," Alice informed the girls, sliding off Sox and landing softly with bended knees.

"I hope you guys don't mind that three of us are joining in today!" she continued, causing Jacqui to smile.

"It'll sure make things interesting!" Jacqui replied.

She didn't mention she was a little nervous about riding with two strangers who were more experienced than she was.

"All ready!" Hannah exclaimed, having tightened the strap on Jasper's girth.

Jacqui hurriedly turned her attention back to Matty, realising she was the only one not ready. *Well, not the only one.* She glanced back up at Alice.

"Alice, where's your saddle?"

"In Tina's float. Her parents drove me here today and I stopped at the paddock to get Sox here quickly so we wouldn't be late. Where should I tie Sox so I can get him ready to ride?" she questioned with a smile.

Following Jacqui's direction, she tied her chestnut gelding to a nearby rail. Then she headed over to the float that the roan gelding had been unloaded from and disappeared around the other side.

"So if these two girls ride at the same level as Alice, will they want to ride in the same lesson as us?" Hannah voiced the question Jacqui had on her mind.

The three girls looked at each other and shrugged. The day had taken an interesting turn!

Kara had obviously thought about the two different riding levels for her class. She put all six girls through a thorough warm up before introducing them to the idea of working in pairs. Each of the older three girls was paired with Jacqui, Geordie and Hannah. They had to safely work beside each other and focus on keeping their horses at the same pace at a walk, trot and even canter.

It took a little while for each rider on the shorter horse to realise they should be travelling on the inside of the pair. This way they didn't have to work as hard to keep up with their longer legged partner.

All six girls worked well together, focusing on communicating with their mount about the speed at which they should be going. Kara deemed the lesson idea a success and finished with the girls having a short relay race. All six finished breathless with delight.

The second lesson involved a version of follow the leader where each rider had to carry out five specific movements whilst in the lead. These could be done in any order, but needed to be communicated to the group of people behind them.

Jacqui found it a bit challenging to think about what she wanted to do, where she wanted to go *and then* remember to communicate this with the other five girls. She had a lot of fun though and found that she was more confident about directing the three older girls by the end of the session. Over lunch the six easily chatted about their morning's ride.

Jacqui found she was relieved that they'd enjoyed themselves and seemed keen to come back the following month. *Genesis has its own riding club! Now we just need to find some more agistees to help the business grow.*

Nine

Kate smiled as she read over the next assignment in the horse course she was undertaking. It was focused around whole farm planning and required that she detail a horse property, what the facilities and paddocks were like and how these could be improved. How fitting that she should be able to do it on Genesis!

She underlined a couple of phrases that weren't familiar to her and jotted down notes about other areas she needed to do. Since coming to the farm almost a year ago, Kate felt that she, Tony and the kids had made some productive changes to the plants and facilities at Genesis.

She was excited to think that an assignment she needed to do for her TAFE course would benefit the family's future plans for the property. Kate had worked out that she could finish her diploma by the end of the year, having received recognition of prior learning for quite a few subjects. As the property improved and she gained a horse qualification, she couldn't help but be optimistic about acquiring more clients for the property and being able to consider working from home full time.

The phone rang suddenly, interrupting her thoughts. She rose from the kitchen table where she'd been sorting through the mail and found her latest assignment.

"King residence, this is Kate," she spoke after picking up the phone.

Kate smiled as their real estate agent introduced themselves.

"What can I do for you, Tim?" she asked, unsure why he would be calling.

"I'm not sure there's anything I need to be asking of you, Kate. I called because the owner of the property has indicated that they would like to put Genesis on the market," Tim informed her.

Kate sat down slowly. *Our home is going up for sale?*

"Is there a set timeframe?" she asked, questioning how much longer they had on their lease before it needed renewing.

"He's told us that he'll happily wait until you've reached the end of your lease. Then the property will go on the market and you'll be able to keep renewing the lease monthly until a buyer is found. Unless..."

"Unless?" Kate questioned, unsure how this unwelcome news could be improved.

"Unless you'd like to make an offer on the property before the end of your lease in June," Tim informed her, waiting quietly on the line.

Kate sighed.

"Thank you for the offer, Tim. I'd love to say it's an option for us and I'll discuss it with my husband, but I'm not sure we could feasibly come up with a substantial deposit before the end of this month," she admitted sadly.

The pair talked for awhile longer, Tim notifying Kate that once a buyer was found, it'd be another 1 – 3 months before settlement would come in and the Kings would need to be relocated. Kate wrote this information down on the notepad she kept by the phone. She was sure Tony would be asking about this later. For now she was only able to process the fact that the property they were dreaming of doing up and generating an income from was to be taken from under them.

As Kate hung up the phone, she questioned what God had in store for the family. She admitted to herself that she would be greatly disappointed if they had to relocate somewhere else for Tony to be able to continue in his position.

"And the kids will be devastated," she murmured to herself, still sitting on the chair.

"But, although it seems impossible to me that we should purchase Genesis, my God can do immeasurably more than I could ever hope or imagine," Kate spoke firmly as she stood.

Lord, that we will find that is the case here. But let it be not about what I want, but Your will for our lives.

Kate glanced at the horse assignment on the table and found she wasn't motivated to get started on it as she had been five minutes ago. She checked the clock and realised the children would be home from school soon.

Needing to feel productive, Kate decided to start on tea early. Perhaps it would take her mind from the sad news she'd just received.

Tony arrived home from work a little flat. Kate loved her children but was glad when the pair was distracted by the television. She finished making herself and her husband a cup of tea before sitting beside him at the table. She hadn't yet had a chance to bring up Genesis being put on the market – she hadn't wanted to alarm the children before she and Tony had had a chance to discuss their options.

"Issues with your manager?" Kate asked, fearing she already knew the answer.

"I'm really struggling to respond positively to the woman when it seems to me that she's unethical and not speaking the truth all the time," Tony sighed, taking a sip from his mug.

"How is she being unethical?" Kate questioned, concerned.

"Nick resigned yesterday afternoon. I hadn't realised that, but Jody called a meeting amongst the four of us and Clarkeson and indicated that Nick would be leaving us in two weeks' time. She then went on to say how the position would be left open for Nick for the next month, should he change his mind and indicated how much help he'd been since she started and how she'd be sorry to see him go. I thought she'd had a change of heart with regards to how she was treating her staff!" Tony commented, squeezing Kate's hand as she took his.

"I looked at Nick and noticed he was really uncomfortable in the meeting. Once Jody and Clarkeson had dismissed us, I suggested to Nick that it was time for our coffee break and perhaps he'd like to have a chat."

"What did he have to say?" Kate asked, concerned where the story was heading.

"He struggled to calm down and managed to tell me in short bursts that when he resigned, Jody had had a very different conversation with him. Nick told me that she'd informed him the position would be easily filled if he felt he was better off elsewhere and that she wouldn't be able to give him a positive reference based on the work she'd seen from him since starting."

Kate sat quietly, dumbfounded.

"I know Nick. He wouldn't lie about anyone, even if he was struggling with getting along with them."

Kate nodded.

"So Nick is still leaving? He's not likely to change his mind and tell Jody he'd like to take her up on the offer of the job still being open?" she asked her husband.

Tony shook his head.

"I challenged him to test her words, to see if she was being genuine but he said based on what she said to him in their one-on-one meeting and how she responded to the situation in front of her manager and her staff, he was certain moving on was the right position. Apart from being angry with how she mishandled the situation, he seems a lot calmer knowing he's not going to be working under her for much longer."

Kate nodded and sighed.

"Poor Nick… how are you feeling about things?"

"Terrible, but I don't see how things can be changed. I'd love to go to Clarkeson and indicate the manipulative game Jody is playing, but I think that's for Nick to do, not for me to go on what he's told me. I think it might be worth me putting out feelers for other jobs, too. If the issues with our manager escalate, I want to be in a position where I can safely walk out to another job, not find myself without work and searching."

Kate's heart took a lurch.

"This sounds like a horrible position to be in, but I think it's wise you look for other work. I guess today just isn't about good news," she sighed.

Tony looked up at his wife.

"The kids seemed fine and the horses were all looking alert when I came down the drive. Is everything ok at your work?" he asked, concerned.

"Work is fine, thank you. I got a call from the real estate agent today..."

Kate went on to detail the phone conversation she'd had with Tim. Tony sat quietly, allowing her to run through what they'd discussed. He got her to repeat how much was being asked for the property and sighed.

"And I'd guess the owner wants at least a ten percent deposit, maybe twenty?" he questioned.

"I'm not actually sure and didn't think to ask. Sorry, honey. I can call Tim back tomorrow if you like."

Tony shook his head.

"Maybe not so soon. I know for a fact that we have less than five percent of what they're asking in our bank account – I can't see how that'd be an appealing deposit for such a large property. To top things off, I don't have the sense that my position is secure even though we moved interstate for me to take it on. I have a feeling that even if we secured funds for a mortgage on our combined wages, it wouldn't be quite enough to make up the other 95%. Nor am I sure the banks would be interested in loaning us so much of the property's value."

Kate nodded and sighed.

"God has blessed us so much with this move. It was shaky at first but it feels like we're just building momentum. I hate the idea that we'd have to share with the kids that we can't stay... then the current agistees may have to find elsewhere to keep their horses... oh!" Kate gasped, "if we have to move then we can't keep Jacob doing odd jobs around the property and know that the Smiths have some income they can rely on weekly."

Tony grabbed Kate's hand.

"They are all valid concerns, but we're not done for yet. Who knows what God will do, or what he has in mind for us. Maybe the job transfer was to put us in a position to meet the Smiths and help them come to know about Christ; maybe it was to get us over here and he has a better job in mind for me; maybe it was for both of those things *and* for us to be able to secure a property like Genesis."

Kate nodded.

"You're right. Tony, if we can do it, I'd love the opportunity to put in an offer on the property."

Tony smiled at his wife.

"Why doesn't that surprise me?" he teased, causing her to frown.

"Would you rather that we find somewhere else to live? Perhaps purchase a house that wouldn't have such a large commitment in the form of a mortgage, or find another place to rent?"

Tony shook his head. Kate sighed, relieved.

"I think tonight my wife; we have a bit of praying to do. I believe we should include the kids in this decision, but perhaps before that we'll work out a game plan. First, let's seek God about this, and then we can work out anything we can actively do to increase our chances of securing the farm if this is where we feel He's leading us. Then we can have a family meeting and let the kids know the news, see what their thoughts are and share our plans with them."

"And perhaps we should share with the Smiths after that. It's not nice news to tell them, but if they're praying and working with us towards a solution, how great a testimony would that be when God works things out for the best of all of us."

Tony smiled.

"I knew I married you for a reason," he commented, kissing her on the cheek.

He paused to listen to the television before checking his watch.

"I think we'd better remind those two what the time is, finish our cuppas and then call it a night."

Kate nodded, more than ready for bed but suddenly refreshed at the idea that things may not look so glum.

Ten

Kate sighed as she filled in the spreadsheet she'd set up for the property. She was creating a business plan for Genesis. She and Tony had prayed the night before and again early the next morning.

The pair had felt that they should be fighting for the property, even though it seemed impossible to acquire by their current savings. Kate had read in her bible that day the verse she'd spoken aloud the afternoon before, about God's provision being more than any human mind could conceive. This had helped her to feel encouraged and determined to make a go of things.

Tony had suggested that she put together a business plan that indicated how many paying agistees they had and how much financially this provided on a monthly basis. After all, this was a third form of income that they could take to the banks when seeking a loan.

The figures were ok, but not as promising as they could be. Kate concluded that the property could feasibly manage 40 – 50 horses on it, if managed well. The income this had the potential to generate would be enough alongside Tony's work to convince the banks that the family had income coming in, to pay a mortgage and support their family.

Kate questioned if any potential clients contacted her in the near future, if this was a positive thing helping the King family to work towards that figure of 40 horses, or if she should indicate that the property may not be available for agistment for much longer. She made a note to talk this over with Tony once he got home from work.

The pair had decided to sit down with Jacqui and Ross that evening and explain what was happening with the property. Kate wasn't looking forward to seeing their disappointment. However, she felt it was important the whole family be aware of the fact that they may need to move.

Jacqui sighed, chewing on her peanut butter sandwich thoughtfully. She'd had another ride on Matty with Kara over the weekend. Kara had insisted that they focus on flat work, rather than jumping. Jacqui had responded that she really wanted to practice her jumping.

The older teen had honestly told Jacqui that they could practice jumping, only if Jacqui were happy to ride Banjo instead of Matty. Kara pointed out that they would have the same issues that they had last jump lesson because of Jacqui's long legs and Matty's short height.

In the end they'd stuck to a flat work lesson, but Jacqui was annoyed and distracted and hadn't communicated well to her pony. She'd ridden home angry and hurt to think that she couldn't do jumps – her favourite thing at the moment – on her favourite pony. Thoughts of needing to send Matty back to Hannah's aunt Jan were increasingly making their way into her head. This made her miserable.

"What's wrong with you? Did someone die?" Geordie asked her blonde friend as she sat down beside Jacqui.

Jacqui looked up in surprise.

"Why would you think someone had died?"

"Well, you seem really unhappy. When my grandma died I think I looked like you do now. So, I assumed that maybe someone had died," Geordie responded simply, causing Hannah to laugh.

"Maybe Jacqui's unhappy about having to send Matty back to Aunt Jan," she suggested, taking a large bite of her apple.

Jacqui looked up quickly. She didn't think anyone else had noticed that she was getting too big for the little bay pony. She looked at Hannah thoughtfully, questioning if her friend was amused by something that was making her so miserable.

"It'll be horrible if you have to send him back soon, but you are getting a bit tall for him, Jacqui," Hannah said sensibly.

Jacqui frowned.

"Then who will I ride?"

"Jasper!" Hannah responded, causing Jacqui to smile at her friend.

"And didn't your mum say that Captain was for the whole family? I'm sure you'd learn a lot riding such a big horse. I'd love to be riding a horse like Captain when I grow too big for Jasper," Hannah continued.

"You think you'll outgrow Jasper?" Jacqui asked in surprise.

She hadn't thought about her friends growing too big for their ponies. After all, Matty was quite a bit shorter than Jasper and Shiela.

"I should say so," Hannah responded simply, "I love him and he's been the most wonderful first pony for me. I'll never forget all that I've learnt from him, but at some point I will grow too big, or my riding will increase to a stage where I can achieve more on a horse. I hope it doesn't happen soon, but I'm pretty sure it will happen!"

Jacqui sat, surprised. She couldn't believe Hannah was being so casual about the idea of giving up her first pony. *Maybe that's because she doesn't have to do it right now.*

"Well I'm going to keep Rose forever," Geordie declared emphatically, causing Hannah to laugh.

"Even if you can't ride her anymore?" Hannah challenged her fiery friend.

"Why not? She could stay at Genesis and keep the other horses company."

"And would you want a new pony to ride?" Jacqui asked, thinking it a lovely idea that Geordie should keep Rose.

"Of course! But that doesn't mean I have to give up Rose."

"Maybe not, but you'll have to do a lot more work at Genesis or get a job to pay for a second pony to be agisted on Jacqui's parents' place," Hannah reasoned.

Geordie frowned.

"I hadn't considered that."

Hannah laughed again.

"Well hopefully you won't have to worry about that for awhile. So what are we focusing on tomorrow night for our study?" she asked Geordie and Hannah.

Caitlin and Amelia soon came to join the girls at lunch and the five discussed the most recent homework they needed to get done. Jacqui was glad for the distraction from her worries.

"Do you two have much homework you need to focus on tonight?" Kate asked her children at the dinner table that night.

Ross shook his head. Jacqui indicated that she didn't either.

"The five of us will do our usual Wednesday catch up after school tomorrow and I'm pretty sure I'll finish the little bit I have to do then. Actually, it's getting a head start on our next assignment. I'm pretty up to date on my schoolwork," she replied, causing her mother to smile.

"That's great honey," Kate responded, looking across the table at Tony.

"Your father and I would like to talk with you two about something. Now that we've finished dinner, do you think we could do that?"

Jacqui shrugged. Ross looked uncomfortable.

"Is everything ok?" he asked, looking from his mother to his father.

Tony sighed.

"We sure hope so. But I'm afraid we have some sad news that we haven't yet found a solution to."

Jacqui frowned, questioning what could be worse than having to give up her pony soon. Ross looked expectantly at his parents.

"I got a call from the real estate agent yesterday," Kate began.

Noting she had Jacqui and Ross' attention, she went over the conversation they'd had. Jacqui gasped at the news.

"We have to give up Genesis?" she asked, ready to cry.

This is even worse than me outgrowing Matty!

"Does that mean Geordie and Hannah have to move their ponies? Oh and Alice! What will we do with Captain?"

Kate took her daughter's hand and squeezed it.

"We don't know yet honey. We're currently considering our options."

"And what are they?" Ross asked, looking to his dad for an answer.

"I don't want to give you both false hope, but your mother and I have decided we want to fight for this property. This means finding money that we don't yet have, to buy it."

"Yes!" Jacqui exclaimed, "So it's all ok?"

71

Kate shook her head.

"We can't guarantee that, Jacqui. What we're saying is that we're going to do everything we can to secure the property and ensure that a situation like this can't arise again. The current owner wants a lot for Genesis and although we may be able to borrow most of this from the bank, we need to prove to the bank that we can pay it back."

"But you and dad both have jobs, isn't that enough?" Ross asked, trying to understand the situation.

"How much we earn determines how much the bank is willing to loan us," Tony clarified, looking at both of his children, "and at the moment the figures we have don't look as good as they need to. We can also claim the money that we earn from agistment as income, so this will help a little."

"So we just need to get more agistees!" Jacqui burst in, grinning at her parents.

"That would make a little difference, yes honey. I'm not sure it's fair to take on more agistees at the moment, though. We can't guarantee that they can stay here long term and they may settle in and then have to move again."

Jacqui sighed.

"So how can we buy Genesis?" she asked, uncertain.

"First, we pray," Kate said firmly, "your father and I believe God has us here for a reason and we don't think it's time for us to go yet. Sometimes when something seems impossible, that's a great opportunity for God to work a miracle and for His people to be able to share what He did."

Jacqui thought about this for a moment.

"I can do that," she declared, determined to start that night.

"Me too," Ross chimed in, "but are there other things that we can do to help out practically?"

Tony smiled at his children.

"Your willingness to pray and your attitudes to this news will help your mother and I greatly! We have 3 weeks until we need to make an offer to the current owner if this is what we find we can do. Whatever money we can put toward our savings over that time will help us, so we may ask that the whole family misses out on some things for the next little while. Every little bit helps."

Ross nodded, saying that he and Jacqui would make a list of things they got on their weekly shop that they could go without. Jacqui looked at her brother, surprised.

She wondered if the idea of moving away from Kara was what had motivated him to do all he could to make a difference about their sudden situation. She smiled, deciding it didn't matter – her brother wanted to stay as much as she did. Now all they had to do was find a way!

Eleven

Jacqui found it hard over the next week to not share her news with Geordie and Hannah. Although she was still devastated about the idea of outgrowing Matty, she felt relieved that they knew she was sad about this and that it would cover the feelings she had about potentially losing her current home.

She questioned if it was lying to her friends – not telling them – and made a note to ask her parents if ever there was a time when it was ok to lie. She didn't think so. She prayed God wouldn't think she was lying when she had been asked by her parents to keep their news just in the family – for now.

Kate and Tony had said there would come a point when they would share the news with all of their current clients. First however, they wanted a chance to focus their energy on finding a way to purchase Genesis.

Jacqui knew her mother had been putting together a business plan and that Tony had applied for more hours at work over the next couple of weeks to be able to earn a little more. For their part, Jacqui and Ross had worked out some items they could give up that would save the family on their weekly food shop. This money would be put towards the deposit they currently had.

Jacqui had raided her piggy bank, desperately hoping that her coins would add up to a significant amount. Ross had laughed at her actions, especially when they counted the total amount to be less than twenty dollars. Jacqui had tersely told her brother that at least she was trying to help!

This had caused him to stop laughing and walk away thoughtfully. Jacqui didn't care what he was up to, she was too busy thinking of things she may be able to sell to have more money to give her parents. *Maybe with me having to give Matty back, I could sell the rug I got for him.* She wondered if it would sell for close to what they'd purchased it for and made a note to ask her mother.

"Why would you want to know how much we might be able to get for Matty's rug?" Kate had asked, surprised by her daughter's question that evening.

"Well if I am going to have to send him back because I'm outgrowing him, I thought we could put the money towards buying Genesis."

Kate smiled sincerely, putting down the knife and carrot that she had been cutting.

"That is a wonderfully generous idea, darling. Both you and Ross have already helped us greatly in working out what you're willing to forego over the next few weeks. Although we would like to have more saved than we currently do, I don't think we should be rushing to sell anything that may bring in a little extra money. Plus, Matty would miss his rug! It's pretty cold during the day, not to mention at night."

Jacqui nodded.

"So I shouldn't think about selling anything?"

Kate shook her head.

"Not at all, honey. What would be more helpful for our situation is that we pray God finds a way to provide your father and I, with a larger income over the long term. This may mean more hours becoming available at my work that I can take on. The banks will be interested in how much we have saved for the farm, but they'll be more interested in how much money we are able to earn each week, as this will show them that we can continue to support our family and pay the banks back the money they loan us."

Jacqui thought this over.

"Ok, I guess we shouldn't sell Matty's rug then. When are you meeting with the bank?"

"Next week. We'll pray as a family the night before even though I'm sure we're all praying each day already!"

Jacqui nodded.

"You bet!"

Jacqui settled down to read a book for school while Kate finished preparing dinner. It was going to be a late meal due to Tony working longer and Ross being over at Kara's to watch a new DVD she'd gotten.

That weekend Alice was down to ride Sox, while her younger sister Megan was led around on Magik by their brother. Another agistee Bob had been about earlier in the day and had offered Jacqui a chance to ride the elder of his three mares.

He'd put Jacqui on the lunge and had her walk, trot and canter. It was the first time the young girl had felt herself truly smiling in a week. She was amazed at the different feel of riding this larger mare that was such a smooth mover. She concluded that as much as she'd miss Matty, maybe it wouldn't be so bad riding on a larger horse.

Jacqui had eagerly told Alice all about the short ride. Alice had listened with interest as she brushed over Sox.

"That sounds great! I really like Bob; he seems to know a lot about horses."

Jacqui nodded, thinking he seemed to know *everything*.

"Tina and Faith really do, too. You know how they're planning to come to the riding club here next moth, right?"

Jacqui nodded. Both girls had indicated they would return when they had taken part in Genesis' riding club for the first time.

"Yeah…"

"Well they suggested to me that they might consider keeping their horses here, too. You see, we all have to float our horses to our current pony club, but I don't need to worry about that with Sox being kept here and the riding club being here. That is really appealing to Tina and Faith and they wonder if it may be worth moving their horses here so that they don't have to travel to another place each month."

Jacqui leant on the rail in the tie up area, staring at Alice. *Two more agistees? Two more agistees!*

She frowned, wondering if her parents would take them on in their current situation. Alice misinterpreted the young girl's look.

"Is that a bad thing? Didn't you like Tina and Faith?" she asked defensively.

Jacqui started.

"Oh, I'm sorry Alice! The girls seemed really nice and I think it'd be wonderful for them to keep their horses here. I guess it'd be worth you talking this over with my mother."

Alice smiled, relieved.

"I'll do that. I think in the end Tina and Faith would need to talk with Kate about it, but I can mention the possibility to her. Is your mother about?"

Jacqui nodded, saying she was in the house but would be out later to hay the horses. Alice said she would ride her gelding and speak with Jacqui's mother later. Jacqui wondered how that conversation would go. She thought maybe she'd better warn her mother so that it wouldn't be a surprise.

She watched Alice walk out to the arena paddock with Sox before heading into the house. She'd already ridden Matty earlier in the day with Geordie and Hannah. Both girls had had to leave early for a party that was being held at the East Riding School. Jacqui had thought she would be lonely without them but found that her afternoon had been easily filled.

She kicked off her boots at the door, calling down the hallway.

"Mum?"

"In the office!" came the reply.

Jacqui walked to the fourth bedroom that her mother had set up with a computer and files for Genesis.

"What's up honey?" Kate asked glancing up from the computer screen as her daughter paused in the doorway.

"Alice is here working Sox... she mentioned that Tina and Faith had really enjoyed the riding club the other week."

Kate nodded.

"They did say they would be coming back again."

"Alice said they also mentioned it may be easier for them to keep their horses here and not have to float them each month. They already have to do that with their pony club..."

Kate sat quietly, digesting the information.

"Alice said she'd talk with you when you feed the horses this afternoon. I thought maybe I should tell you so you have time to work out what to say to her."

Kate smiled fondly at her daughter.

"That's very thoughtful of you, Jacqui. Thank you."

The young girl headed back outside, Kate smiling at the news. Although it wasn't certain that they could continue to offer agistment, she loved that God was providing potentially two new clients. She prayed that they would be able to take them on.

Tony came home the following week in a cheery mood. Kate was surprised but pleased. He chattered away with Ross and Jacqui, joking with the pair. Kate laughed as

Ross rolled his eyes at a particularly bad joke Tony had made.

"That's terrible, dad. If you're going to tell such bad jokes, I think I'd rather be watching telly," he declared, rising from the table to put his plate in the dishwasher.

Jacqui agreed, following her brother. Kate laughed as Tony looked at her and shrugged with a silly grin on his face.

"What did I say?" he asked, causing her to laugh again.

"You seem so happy tonight. Work was good, I take it?"

"It was a relief, honestly. The day was reasonable with Jody and tense at times, but the overtime was a delight. I'd forgotten how much I enjoyed my job before this new manager came along. Is that a bad thing?"

Kate shook her head.

"I'm glad God has given you an opportunity to remember what you loved about the position in the first place. I'm just sad that the reminder was necessary and that most of your hours are not like the overtime you've picked up."

Tony nodded.

"Me too. I'm so thankful for the opportunity to work a little more based on our current financial desires. I'm not sure that I want to continue working under this woman, however. I'd really like some direction from God on this. I thought finding another job was worth considering, but if we want to secure Genesis, then another job is out of the question."

Kate sighed.

"We definitely need to seek guidance on that one. It's obvious the kids want to stay here, too."

Kate detailed the conversation she'd had with Jacqui about selling Matty's rug. Tony laughed.

"That's such a lovely idea. It's a pity his rug isn't lined with gold," he joked.

"A pity indeed," Kate agreed.

The pair caught up on each others' day before heading into the lounge room to watch an early movie with their children. It had become a bit of a tradition on Tuesday nights.

Twelve

Jacqui and Ross met their parents at the door, eager for good news. Kate smiled when she saw them, unsure how to tell them.

"So?" they both asked eagerly.

"How about you let your mother and I inside from this freezing weather before we get into a lengthy discussion," Tony advised firmly, rubbing his hands together in the cold.

The pair meekly stood aside, letting their parents pass. Kate asked Ross to put on the kettle as she took her coat off and hung it by the door. With a sigh the teen headed into the kitchen quickly, flicking the switch. Jacqui raced after him, eager to get mugs out. The sooner they had their parents comfortably settled, the sooner they'd find out if buying Genesis was an option.

Jacqui carried in a mug of cocoa for each of her parents while Ross brought in one for himself and his sister. They sat on the floor before their parents, who were seated on the couch. Kate looked to Tony, unsure who should start. He smiled and turned his attention to their kids.

"I'm sorry to say we can't give you good news from the banks," Tony told the pair, warming his hands around the mug.

"At the moment your mother and I just don't earn enough for them to consider loaning us the amount we'd need to buy Genesis."

Ross sighed, taking a sip from his cup. Jacqui put hers down beside her; she didn't want a hot cocoa anymore.

"So someone else can buy Genesis?" she asked, her voice small.

"Potentially, honey. I'm due to call the real estate agent tomorrow to let him know if we can consider putting an offer on the property. Unfortunately because we can't, it will mean that the current owner puts it up for sale."

The rest of the conversation Jacqui forgot to pay attention to. What did it matter? Genesis was going to be available for someone else to buy. They would have to move.

She was angry that God would allow something like this to happen. First she'd outgrown Matty in a short space of time and then He'd not let them keep the property where her friends were keeping their horses and where she was living. It wasn't fair!

By mid July all the agistees had been informed about the situation. Kate was surprised and pleased to find that each horse owner was happy to keep their horses on the property until they were required to move. She hadn't expected the loyalty and yet when she questioned it, she realised that God had provided a blessing in this area, too.

She knew she should never question His character or provision. The longer the agistees stayed on the property, the longer she and Tony could save.

The paperwork had been sorted between the real estate agent and the current owner that week. Genesis was now officially on the market.

Young Tina and Faith had approached Kate about agisting on the property. She'd informed them about the sale of Genesis and indicated that although they were more than welcome to keep their horses on the property, it may not appeal to their parents to potentially have to relocate in a short space of time.

Tina and Faith's parents had agreed, leaving the two teenagers disappointed. Thankfully their parents were happy for them to continue coming to Genesis' riding club and to float the horses there. For this Kate was thankful.

The following riding club was a bittersweet moment. Everyone was aware that it could be one of their last moments to ride together and learn from each other. To make matters worse for Jacqui, she was sending Matty back to Hannah's Aunt Jan. This was her last riding club with the responsive little bay pony. She was just too tall to continue riding him.

The Saturday after riding club, Kate borrowed a float from Alice's parents. With Jacqui's help, she loaded Matty for the drive up north. Ross had started a part time job that week and been asked if he could cover the morning shift because another staff member was sick. He'd been ecstatic to learn that if he worked on a weekend, he earnt more per hour.

Kate was pleased that her son was taking on a responsibility that would help him to learn the value of money. She made a note to talk with him about finding a balance between study, a part time job and time with family.

There was also the question of what he would choose to do with the money he earnt. Both Jacqui and Ross knew that their parents gave an offering each week at church, but Kate wasn't sure if Ross realised that the offering was a small way for them to thank God for the abundance He gave the family.

Jacqui sat quietly in the car as they made their way down the nearby freeway. Kate knew that her daughter was hurting a lot.

"What are Geordie and Hannah up to today?" she asked, keen to talk with her.

Jacqui shrugged.

"No riding?" Kate persisted.

"I don't think so. I think Amelia and Caitlin are with them seeing the latest horror movie. I don't like movies that make me scared," Jacqui responded.

Kate nodded her head before indicating that she was exiting the freeway. She glanced in her mirror to make sure there was plenty of room to change lanes with a float attached to the car.

"I think it's wise to avoid watching or hearing things that makes us feel bad. God can speak to us through movies and music, but so can the enemy."

"And does God speak to us through taking away the things that are most dear to us?" Jacqui asked suddenly, a hint of bitterness in her voice.

85

Kate was surprised to hear such a tone from her daughter. She decided not to reprimand her, aware of her hurt.

"God does many things we can't understand, Jacqui. But that doesn't mean He doesn't care for us. In fact, often the things that He lets happen, help us to grow closer to Him and learn to rely on Him. It's about letting God have free reign in our lives."

"Free rein? Like the reins on a bridle?" Jacqui asked, confused.

"Not quite honey. A king reigns over his people and land. It's spelt with a silent G in it. R.e.i.g.n. Letting God reign in our lives means that we accept that He is in control through the good and bad. It means that we put our entire trust in Him, not in the things that are going on around us."

"But why would He let Genesis get sold? And why do I have to give up Matty so soon?"

"It is a shame that Matty isn't taller," Kate agreed, "and although we didn't expect you to outgrow him so soon, I don't think we can blame God for the fact that Matty is a short pony and you're going to be a tall young woman. There's no way I'd be small enough to still ride the first few ponies that I learnt on!"

Jacqui sighed. Kate glanced at her daughter with a small smile.

"At least we know that Matty is going back to his home where he can spend time with ponies he knows and a great horse owner. I'm sure Jan will look after him."

"Oh, I know she will. I just wish it was me looking after him still."

"In a way you are," Kate responded, causing her daughter to look at her in confusion.

"You are looking after him by choosing to miss out on riding him because you're getting too tall. You're also sending him back to a woman who knows how to care for him. That's looking after Matty too."

Jacqui thought this over. She decided she had to agree with her mother.

"I guess... and God letting Genesis go up for sale?" she asked, hoping Kate would be able to point out the good in that situation to her.

Kate sighed.

"I honestly don't know, honey. All I know is our God is incredible, He loves us more than we could ever imagine and He has our best interests at heart. I don't know what is going to happen, but I do know that God will look after us, no matter what."

"Because... you've let Him have free reign in your life?" Jacqui asked dubiously.

"Because that's who God is," Kate clarified, "His character doesn't change. It's when I accept His control over my life that I find I change. I'm happier, even when I'm uncertain about the future."

Kate stopped talking, thinking she'd given her daughter a lot to think about. Jacqui sat quietly in the car, looking out the window at the tall buildings. They'd reached the city. She couldn't believe how big the buildings were.

Within an hour they'd managed to get out of the city and head down the Hume highway. Paddocks were becoming more common on either side of the road. Jacqui preferred this view, especially if there was a horse or two in them.

She thought over what her mother had said as she gazed out of the window. She wasn't sure she could change her hurt for acceptance. It didn't seem fair that God had allowed two big changes that upset her to happen in her life. She knew He was all powerful and loved her, but couldn't see how He was demonstrating that at the moment. Confused, she fell asleep in the car.

All too quickly Kate was calling gently to her daughter to awaken her. Jacqui opened her eyes, wiping at them as she tried to awaken fully.

"We're here," Kate said softly.

Jacqui looked around quickly as she heard Matty move in the horse float behind them. *Here already!* Jacqui sighed.

"I wish we didn't have to return him, mum."

"I know honey. Perhaps it's good that it's happening at a time when we may not have somewhere to keep him anymore though."

Jacqui didn't see any good in that, or having to return Matty. It all seemed bad to her. She didn't respond. As Kate undid her seatbelt and got out of the car, Jacqui followed.

Jan came out of the house and indicated that they could unload the little bay pony where they had stopped. Jacqui opened the side door to the float and hopped in to untie Matty. She knew that until she'd done that and told her mother, Kate wouldn't lower the back ramp.

"We're ready!" she called out, hoping her mum would hear although she was talking with Jan.

Jacqui heard the bolts being opened on the float and then saw daylight as the ramp was slowly lowered. Matty waited patiently until Jacqui let him know it was ok to back off the large trailer. She patted his neck, thinking again how wonderful a first pony he had been.

"I doubt I could find a pony better than you," she said fiercely, putting pressure on his chest so that he knew he could start backing away from her.

Kate had opened the tailgate and it was clear for the pony to exit. He did so at a safe pace, looking around with alert ears as Jacqui stepped off the float with him.

He let out a shrill whinny, moving his feet impatiently. Jan laughed.

"I don't think he's forgotten this place!"

A few ponies called in reply. Jacqui smiled in spite of herself. It was a lovely sound.

"So young Jacqui, do you remember where the pony paddock is?" Jan asked of the blonde girl.

"Of course!" Jacqui responded, surprised.

Jan smiled.

"Wonderful. Well I remember how capable you are with horses and I can only imagine that that has improved since I saw you last. How about you take Matty to the pony paddock and remove his halter and lead so that he can join his friends?"

Jacqui nodded, turning the bay pony towards his old paddock.

"One more thing," Jan called out, causing Jacqui to pause.

"Since you were here last I've made a small change to their paddock. There are now two gates to walk through before Matty will be with his friends. If you open the first gate and go inside, then you can close it after you and remove his head collar and lead rope. Then you can open up the second gate and allow him to head out to his friends."

Jacqui nodded, wondering why two gates were necessary. Jan smiled as she saw this question on the young girl's face.

"I'm not sure if you've let a horse back into a paddock full of horses after it's been away for awhile, Jacqui?" Jan questioned.

Jacqui shook her head, indicating that she hadn't.

"They can get so excited by an old friend! Or even a new one. This way it means you can safely release Matty without being surrounded by ponies that sometimes squeal and kick."

Jacqui looked to the older woman, surprised.

"Because of the new gate, I'm sure you'll be fine and safe. Your mother and I are going to go inside and get some hot drinks. You're welcome to join us once Matty is secure in the paddock."

Jacqui nodded, turning her attention back to her walk with the pony. Kate and Jan headed toward the house.

"I guess she's pretty disappointed about outgrowing Matty so soon," Jan commented as she pulled out three mugs from a kitchen cupboard.

Kate nodded.

"That's for sure. There's no way around it though, and we may not have a property to keep any horses at soon, so I feel that it's the right time to be returning him."

Jan looked across to Kate sitting at the kitchen table.

"No more Genesis?" she questioned, putting some sugar into the mugs.

"I'm not sure, Jan. It's being put on the market and unfortunately we're not quite in a position to put an offer on it."

Jan sighed.

"I guess it'd be pointless me raising the idea of Jacqui leasing another pony from me then," she commented, pulling milk out of the fridge.

"Another horse?" Kate asked, surprised.

"Indeed. One that truly would take the sting off her having to return Matty."

"Well now I'm intrigued. If we had land to keep horses, what did you have in mind?"

"I had a grey pony return to the property when the three girls were last here," Jan started.

Kate smiled in recognition.

"Jaq," she cut in, aware of Jacqui's fascination with the grey gelding.

"The one and only. I've been working with him on a regular basis and he's quietened and matured a lot. On top of that, he's a few hands taller than Matty. I don't see with

Jacqui's physique that she'd outgrow or become too heavy for him any time soon."

Kate smiled, taking the warm mug of tea offered to her.

"Plus, with the riding club that Hannah told me has been started at Genesis, I'm sure Jacqui would improve right along with the horse. Perhaps they could even entertain the idea of starting in the show ring. I know the horse will win ribbons from his looks and movement."

"That sounds wonderful, Jan. I wish we were in a position to accept."

Jan shrugged, sipping at her tea.

"Who knows what the future holds? Let me know if the situation on the farm changes. I'm sure you'd once again have a very excitable and overjoyed daughter."

Kate nodded, knowing this to be true. She also knew that Jacqui needed to find joy in other matters if the situation didn't turn around.

Jacqui joined the two women in the house shortly after. She told Jan how much she thought the double gate system was a great idea.

"I hadn't realised the other ponies would be so excited to see Matty!" she explained, eyes wide.

Jan smiled as she described the sniffs and squeals that went on as soon as Matty was allowed to join his friends.

"I'd wanted to say hello and pat the others, but I didn't feel it was a good time to do so," Jacqui admitted shyly.

"Good girl. I like that horse sense about you. You can always do that before you two head back home. And of course you three girls still need to visit again and get some more hours in the saddle on different ponies."

Jacqui smiled shyly, saying she'd have to remind Hannah and Geordie. Although the day was a sad one, Jacqui found her spirits had lifted on the drive home.

Thirteen

Genesis had been on the market a month before someone came to look at the property to buy. Kate's disappointment was felt as strongly as the children's. She tried to put on a brave face as she told them that tidying up the house was important for a possible future buyer.

The same was said for the property. They made sure that all horse gear was put away and the stack of hay bales looked tidy. Although the buyer came on a Saturday and there were agistees making use of the facilities, Kate insisted that Tony take Jacqui with him to Ross' soccer game.

Their daughter had protested strongly. She wanted to be around when the potential buyer came to see the property. Thankfully Kara was attending the soccer match to see Ross play. This, in the end, was the point that made Jacqui agree to go.

Kate stayed out of the way as the agent took their client through the property, pointing out facilities. She couldn't help but feel that some of the selling points were additions that she and Tony had put in, and that the kids had helped to make. *I guess that's what happens when you invest in someone else's property,* she thought.

She was both relieved and incredibly curious when the visitors left. It wasn't fun not knowing what would happen with what could be their future home.

A few more potential buyers came to see the property over the next couple of weeks. Jacqui found herself telling Geordie and Hannah about each visitor that was due. Her two friends would be eagerly waiting the next day at school to hear any updated news. It wasn't a lot of fun.

Kate felt the same way. She found herself praying to God that He would make it known to the King family what would happen, one way or another. It would be horrible to lose Genesis, but it felt worse not knowing and bearing disappointment each time the agent called to indicate someone would be coming to look at the property.

In spite of the unappealing situation, the family worked hard to keep up a routine. Horses were fed; work was done, school work completed and family time sought out.

Jacqui invested much of her energy in watching Geordie and Hannah practice what they learnt at the East Riding School in their fortnightly lessons. She was thrilled to also be able to ride Bob's big grey mare a couple more times.

The older gentleman took great joy in teaching her how to sit proudly astride the mare and develop a sound seat at the sitting trot. Jacqui's riding was improving under his guidance and encouragement. Kara said as much whenever they had a lesson together and Jacqui was on Banjo.

Jacqui was thrilled for the praise; she just wondered sadly if her riding would stop altogether soon. She made a note to ask her parents if that would happen if they moved on from Genesis. Kate was shocked by the question.

"I don't want you to think you have to give up horses altogether if we move homes, Jacqui. I believe we can still keep Captain; we'll just need to find another place for him to live. Plus, I believe Kara would be devastated to lose you as a student. Ask her, but I think she'd want to continue teaching you, even if you lived elsewhere. And of course your father or I would be happy to drive you over to Kara's for your lessons."

Jacqui smiled, relieved. She told her mother she was going to join Ross on a walk with Jack, their kelpie. Kate nodded, distracted as the phone rang.

She answered it and smiled, pleased to find Cindy on the other end of the line.

"I just had to call! I had a dream last night about your property," Cindy said excitedly.

Kate smiled sadly at the words *your property*. She listened as Cindy detailed things that would happen on the property in the future; the Kings still living there. Kate pondered Cindy's dream as she prepared dinner.

She glanced at the clock and frowned. It was getting dark and the children would be inside soon. Tony should have been home half an hour ago. She prayed that everything was ok at work.

Tony arrived home twenty minutes later, sweeping his wife up in a hug. She laughed in delight, surprised by his energy and obvious happiness.

"I was wondering if things were ok! What's going on?" she asked.

"I had a last minute meeting with Clarkeson that I wasn't expecting. It turns out that Jody has been offered a management position elsewhere that she's keen to take on. She's handed in her resignation."

Kate headed into the kitchen with her husband, processing this information. She glanced out the kitchen window to see Ross and Jacqui heading through the gate of the house paddock, Jack leaping excitedly at their legs. She smiled.

"So who's going to head things up?" she questioned curiously.

"That's what he wanted to talk to me about. Clarkeson has asked if I would consider taking on a more managerial role!"

"Would that mean more pressure on you at work?" Kate asked, turning off the oven where their tea had been kept warm.

"It would mean more responsibility. But it would also mean a higher rate of pay and a company car," Tony replied, smiling as his wife caught his eye.

"A promotion?" she questioned in shock.

Tony smiled and nodded.

"If I want it, yes."

"That's amazing!" Kate replied with a smile, pulling the plates out of the oven and setting them at the table.

Jacqui and Ross came in the door then, leaving their boots in the hallway. Kate directed them both to wash their hands as they followed their noses to the table instead.

"You can eat after you've washed your hands," she reminded them with a grin.

Both sighed, heading toward the bathroom. Kate laughed, knowing they would hurry if they were hungry.

The following evening Kate and Tony decided to share the good news with their children. Ross had rolled his eyes as his father made a really bad joke over dinner.

"Dad! That's terrible, I'm so glad you don't say things like that out in public. I'd be so embarrassed," he complained, taking a sip of his drink.

"But Kara loves my jokes!" Tony protested, winking at Jacqui.

Jacqui laughed.

"That's true!" she said, agreeing with her father.

"So your mother and I have some good news," Tony changed the subject.

Jacqui and Ross looked up expectantly. Jacqui wondered if it could be about the property.

"What is it?" Ross asked, pausing from eating his meal.

"I've been offered a promotion at work and have decided to take it."

Ross grinned.

"What's a promotion?" Jacqui asked, thinking this didn't sound like good news about Genesis after all.

"It's something that can happen at work to put you in a higher level of a job," Tony explained.

Jacqui frowned, not following.

"Think of it like you going up a grade in school, Jacqui. As you get older, it's expected that you'll go into the next grade and the work you do will be a bit harder."

Jacqui thought about this and nodded.

"So it's good news that your work will be harder?" she asked, confused.

Tony smiled.

"It may not sound like it, but yes. When you work, you get paid. When you're asked to work harder, you sometimes get paid more or offered other things to reward you for your hard work."

"So you're getting a raise?" Ross asked, grinning again.

Tony smiled and nodded. Noting Jacqui's confusion, he answered her brother's question in a way that would be clearer for her.

"Yes, they're offering to pay me more if I take on this new level of work. They're also offering a work vehicle that I can use during the week which will save us money because we don't have to use our car as often."

"That's great!" Ross responded, ready to continue with his meal.

Jacqui nodded, smiling at her parents.

"I thought you were going to say something about us being able to get Genesis," she admitted shyly, "but that is good news, dad."

Tony smiled warmly at his daughter.

"Actually Jacqui, this promotion at work means that we may be able to get Genesis. Because I will be earning more money, the banks are likely to let us borrow more money. Your mother and I will go back to them to find out if we can buy Genesis."

Jacqui put her fork of beans down, staring at her father in surprise.

"Really?" she asked in a small voice, not daring to believe it.

"Really," Kate responded, squeezing her daughter's hand.

"We'll find out at the end of this week if it's a possibility," Tony told his children, glad to see their excited faces.

The family finished their meal quickly, excitedly talking about what it would mean if they could indeed purchase the property. When Tony suggested they go out for dessert to celebrate, Jacqui and Ross were only too happy to agree.

Over the next two weeks Jacqui and Ross' father accepted and started his new role. The promotion meant that the Kings were in a position to go back to the banks and see if they could buy Genesis.

Jacqui and Ross had been delighted to find that their parents were able to put in an offer on the property. Jacqui was so excited; she didn't know how she would manage to wait to see if her parents' offer had been accepted.

Luckily for her, the time went quickly and she was able to soon share some incredible news with Geordie and Hannah. The Saturday that the family were able to put a 'sold' sticker on the sale sign out the front of Genesis, was one of delight for all.

Kate insisted on getting a photo with the family standing in front of it. Jacqui had laughed in delight as Geordie and Hannah asked to be in the photo and then suggested that they put the horses in it too. The afternoon turned into a happy celebration filled with lots of laughs and ponies, of course!

About the Author

Christine Meunier considers herself introduced to the wonderful world of horses at the late age of 13 when her parents agreed to lease a horse for her. She started experiencing horses via books from a young age and continues to do so, but recognises that horses cannot be learnt solely from books.

She has been studying horses from age 16, starting with the Certificate II in Horse Studies. She completed the Bachelor of Equine Science in 2015.

Christine has worked at numerous thoroughbred studs in Australia as well as overseas in Ireland for a breeding season.

She then gained experience in a couple of Melbourne based horse riding schools, instructing at a basic level before heading off overseas again, this time to South Africa to spend hours in the saddle of endurance and trail horses on the Wild Coast.

Particularly passionate about the world of breeding horses, she writes a blog about equine education which you can view at http://equus-blog.com/

You can contact Christine via email at christine@christinemeunierauthor.com.

Sign up to her author news and receive updates – and freebies – as they are available! http://eepurl.com/bAiMpL

Every effort is made to ensure that this book is free of spelling and grammatical errors. That said, I am only human! If you find any errors, I'd love to know so that I can correct them. You can contact me at christine@christinemeunierauthor.com with details of any issues you may find.

Printed in Great Britain
by Amazon

77548243R00068